Barth's Doctrine of Creation

Creation, Nature, Jesus, and the Trinity

Andrew K. Gabriel

CASCADE *Books* · Eugene, Oregon

BARTH'S DOCTRINE OF CREATION
Creation, Nature, Jesus, and the Trinity

Cascade Books
An Imprint of Wipf and Stock Publishers
199 W. 8th Ave., Suite 3
Eugene, OR 97401

www.wipfandstock.com

ISBN 13: 978-1-62032-954-2

Cataloguing-in-Publication Data

Gabriel, Andrew K.

Barth's doctrine of creation : creation, nature, Jesus, and the Trinity / Andrew K. Gabriel

x + 118 p. ; 23 cm. Includes bibliographical references and indexes.

ISBN 13: 978-1-62032-954-2

1. Barth, Karl, 1886–1968. 2. Barth, Karl, 1886–1968—Contributions to the doctrine of creation. 3. Creation—History of doctrines—20th century. 4. Trinity. I. Title

BT111.3 G20 2014

Manufactured in the U.S.A.

Revisions of the following works appear in this book and are used by permission of the publishers:

Gabriel, Andrew K. "Beyond Anthropocentrism in Barth's Doctrine of Creation: Searching for a Theology of Nature." *Religious Studies and Theology* 28.2 (2009) 175–187.

Gabriel, Andrew K. "A Trinitarian Doctrine of Creation? Considering Barth as a Guide." *McMaster Journal of Theology and Ministry* 6 (2005) 36–48.

Barth's Doctrine of Creation

To my first educators, Mom and Dad,
with love and gratitude

Contents

Acknowledgments

THIS PROJECT, THOUGH SHORT, has been many years in the making. I am thankful for Adrian Langdon, Don Schweitzer, Kurt Anders Richardson, Travis Kroeker, and Clark Pinnock, who have each offered numerous constructive comments and insightful questions at various stages in its progress. On account of their contributions this book is far better than it otherwise would have been. Thanks also to members of the Canadian Theological Society as well as the Canadian Evangelical Theological Association for their comments on my presentation of earlier drafts of some of the material published here.

I am also grateful for the faculty, staff, and students at Horizon College and Seminary, who make the institution such a wonderful place to serve. I thank especially our President (previously Academic Dean), Jeromey Martini, for his thoughtfulness in assuring that I could have the time to complete this project. Thanks also to Ron Kadyschuk for constantly encouraging me in my research and to Leanne Bellamy for applying her keen eye in English to my work.

My deepest appreciation goes to my wife, Krista, for all her love and support. Thanks are also due to our children—Adelyn, Mylah, and Rayelle—who bring much joy to our lives. To use Barth's words, my family serves as a daily

Acknowledgments

reminder of the brighter side of creation and of God's "Yes" to creation. Finally, I thank God for his provision, for all the supportive people God has placed around me during this project, and for giving me the opportunity to see this book come to completion. I pray that it will strengthen our faith in the Creator.

1

Introduction

W HY STUDY KARL BARTH'S doctrine of creation? In
the context of theological studies any discussion of
Barth's work is justified simply because he is repeatedly
recognized as one of the most influential Christian theologians of the twentieth century. Pope Pius XII labeled him
the greatest theologian since Thomas Aquinas. High praise
for a Protestant theologian!

More specifically, Barth's doctrine of creation in
particular merits discussion because of the unique role
that it plays within the history of Christian approaches to
this doctrine. Throughout the history of theology areas
of thought outside of dogmatics have significantly shaped
the doctrine of creation. As a result those developing the
doctrine often neglected the central doctrine of Christianity—a Trinitarian understanding of salvation—and its
significance for the doctrine of creation. In the doctrine's
incipient stages and through to the Middle Ages, it was not

unusual for theologians to relate the doctrine of creation to the doctrine of salvation and recognize creation as a Trinitarian act. However, even during the early patristic period, Greek philosophical understandings of the world often had a determinative influence on the doctrine of creation.[1] As various philosophies continued to influence the doctrine throughout history, many eventually came to believe that the doctrine belonged primarily to this domain. As Hugo Meynell notes, people would "build up a doctrine of creation on philosophical grounds, which is then shown to correspond, as far as it goes, with Christian doctrine, and thus to be useful in commending or confirming it."[2] Following Isaac Newton (seventeenth century) and into the modern era, in wider Western culture the primary foundation for understanding creation switched from the domain of philosophy to science. Here the Trinity seemed no more relevant for understanding creation than within philosophy. Likewise, even aside from wider Western culture, in post-Reformation theology the Trinity became "largely irrelevant to the doctrine of creation."[3] Subsequently, during the nineteenth century, theologians tended to employ forms of pantheism and panentheism. These ideas came with a rejection of historical articulations of the doctrine of the Trinity.

For many, Barth's doctrine of creation marks a return (perhaps even *the return*) to a Trinitarian approach to the doctrine of creation.[4] He focuses more on why there is a creation than how creation originated. His doctrine is not a

1. Gunton, *Triune Creator*, 42.

2. Meynell, *Grace versus Nature*, 143.

3. Gunton, *Triune Creator*, 154. On these time periods see 125–30 and 154–56.

4. Jenson, "Karl Barth," 47; Aung, *Doctrine of Creation*, 2; and Gunton, *Triune Creator*, 157.

protology of the world. Rather, he emphasizes that creation is a result of the will and love of God and that, accordingly, it is directed toward the covenant. In doing so Barth attempts to move beyond dependence upon science or a particular philosophy by presenting a doctrine of creation based upon the Christian faith. As in all of his theology, Barth wishes to start with the God who is revealed in Jesus Christ.

The importance of Barth's doctrine of creation also becomes apparent as one considers the theologies of all of those who have written after him. Just as he has been influential in so many other areas of theology, theologians working on the doctrine of creation are likewise compelled to wrestle with Barth's explication of this doctrine—so much so that Per Lønning observes that to "a large extent current issues in the theology of creation reflect advocacy versus questioning of the Barthian inheritance."[5] For example, H. Paul Santmire's long quest for a theology of nature and an ecologically responsible theology commenced with his doctoral dissertation focusing on Barth's doctrine of creation.[6] Likewise, Jürgen Moltmann's ecological and pneumatological doctrine of creation begins by setting out guidelines for his work, which is in large part a response to Barth's presentation of the doctrine.[7]

CONTEXT OF BARTH'S PROJECT

Barth was born in Basel on May 10, 1886. He grew up in a Swiss Protestant home worshiping within the Reformed

5. Lønning, *Creation*, 13.

6. Santmire, "Creation and Nature." Santmire's dissertation was followed by his *Brother Earth, Travail of Nature, Nature Reborn,* and *Ritualizing Nature.*

7. Moltmann, *History and the Triune God,* 125–42; and Moltmann, *God in Creation,* 1–19.

tradition, and his father was a New Testament and church history professor. He went on to study theology, during which time he was trained under the liberalism of professors Adolf von Harnack and Wilhelm Herrmann. After pastoring from 1910–21, primarily in Safenwil, Switzerland, Barth taught at the German universities of Göttingen, Münster, and Bonn (1921–35). On account of his criticism of Nazism, he was forced by the German government to return to Switzerland, where he taught at Basel until his retirement (1962). He passed away six years later in 1968.[8] His most influential work, *Kirchliche Dogmatik* (*Church Dogmatics*), was written over a long span of years, from 1932–67. He composed his doctrine of creation (in volume III/1 of his *Church Dogmatics*) during WWII, publishing it in 1945, only a few months after the war had ended.

The political situation of the day had a definite impact on Barth. In 1914 Barth found his teachers' embrace of Kaiser Wilhelm's war policy to be an ethical failure, and he accordingly questioned their theology: "Their exegetical and dogmatic presuppositions could not be in order. . . . A whole world of exegesis, ethics, dogmatics and preaching, which I had hither to held to be essentially trustworthy, was shaken to the foundations, and with it, all the other writings of the German theologians."[9] Barth subsequently rejected liberalism and, in contrast to many of his teachers, became part of the Confessing Church in Germany.[10]

8. For an in depth account of Barth's life see Busch, *Karl Barth*.

9. Barth, quoted in Busch, *Karl Barth*, 81. Cf. Busch, *Great Passion*, 19.

10. For an account of how Barth's theology developed throughout his career see McCormack, *Karl Barth's Critically Realistic Dialectical Theology*.

With respect to his more mature theology, Barth focuses on the revelation of Jesus Christ. On the one hand, his theology is a response to existentialism, which he had studied especially in the works of Søren Kierkegaard. Barth found existential theology subjective and found objectivity in Jesus Christ. On the other hand, his theology is also a response to the natural theology of Enlightenment liberalism. Such theology conflated divine and human nature—a modern version of the classic *analogia entis* (analogy of being)—and therefore concluded that God can be known by use of human reason in the construction of theological concepts. Barth rejected any *analogia entis* because, he attests, the revelation of the Word of God does not need justification from the creature through natural theology.[11] Hence, Barth's doctrine of creation, as with the rest of his theology, focuses on the revelation of God in Jesus Christ and, therefore, has a decidedly christological emphasis.

OVERVIEW

Barth studies is burgeoning. And yet Kurt Richardson observes that "*CD* III [Barth's doctrine of creation] is only beginning to receive the treatment it deserves."[12] Monographs that are giving more attention to Barth's doctrine of creation are generally comparative—relating Barth's ideas to those of other theologians or philosophers—rather than

11. *CD* I/1, xiii, 166; II/1, 83–84; III/2, 220; and Barth, *Holy Spirit*, 5. While Balthasar (*Theology of Karl Barth*, 163–64, 382) and others have suggested that Barth eventually changed his mind about the *analogia entis*, Johnson (*Karl Barth and the* Analogia Entis, 158–230) persuasively argues that Barth continued to reject the *analogia entis* throughout his career. Cf. McCormack, "Karl Barth's Version of an 'Analogy of Being,'" 88–144.

12. Richardson, *Reading Karl Barth*, 17.

focused on Barth's contribution in and of itself. This book furthers the exploration of Barth's work (additional work is certainly required) by focusing on his doctrine of creation (especially as found in *Church Dogmatics* III/1 on "The Work of Creation") as well as on how interpreters of Barth have portrayed this aspect of his work. My first aim, then, is to introduce and clarify Barth's doctrine of creation. In addition, I mine insights from Barth that can contribute to a theology of nature or ecological theology and a Trinitarian theology of creation.

In the next chapter I offer an overview of the key points in Barth's doctrine of creation. This includes a discussion of what exactly creation is according to Barth, how he presents the doctrine as distinctly an article of faith, what creation implies regarding the Creator, Barth's creation/covenant thesis, as well as some of his additional emphases.

The following chapters address three recurring critiques of Barth's doctrine of creation. I find value in aspects of those critiques, but also identify ways in which his theology sometimes adequately addresses those critiques. Chapter 3 discusses how many interpreters critique Barth for focusing on humanity to the neglect of nature, that is, all non-human creation. As a result, many claim that his doctrine cannot address the ecological crisis. Nevertheless, within his doctrine one finds insights that can aid those developing a theology of nature, especially within his observation that the whole of creation participates in the covenant.

Barth is often credited with starting a revival of contemporary Trinitarian theology, yet some critique the Trinitarian approach he takes within his doctrine of creation. This is the subject of chapter 4. Although this critique has validity, Barth's theology does illustrate that a Trinitarian doctrine of creation will recognize the relational character of "the image of God," the immanence of God, and that creation and salvation are both the work of the same triune God.

Chapter 5 evaluates how interpreters critique Barth for neglecting the significance of history in forming his doctrine of creation because he focuses on the eternal and pre-temporal Jesus Christ rather than upon the created reality that God and humanity face. This critique is overturned given that he finds knowledge of creation in the historical Jesus Christ and when one considers the historical meaning of covenant in his theology.

2

Contours of Barth's Doctrine of Creation

BEFORE ONE CAN EVALUATE critiques interpreters make of Barth's doctrine of creation, one must first grasp the contours of his doctrine. Hence, this chapter expounds the key points in this aspect of his theology. In summary, for Barth, knowledge of creation is an article of faith. From this article of faith believers learn of the free and loving Creator who has created the world out of nothing for the covenant. This covenantal relationship leads Barth to affirm that creation is distinct from God and that creation is good.

WHAT IS CREATION?

"Creation" can mean more than one thing. Creation is, in a certain sense, a "thing." It is all that is distinct from

God. This includes not just the physical universe, but both heaven and earth, the invisible and the visible. Barth explicitly states that "all that exists is either the Creator Himself or else His creature—God or creation."[1] However, in most instances, Barth's references to "creation" describe an *act* of God, and this tendency is reflected in the title of volume III/1 of his *Church Dogmatics*: "The Work of Creation."

As an act of God, Barth regards creation to be a completed act. God created "in the beginning." The completion of this act is marked by God's Sabbath rest.[2] Barth does not deny the concept of *creatio continua*, but for him this concerns providence rather than a continuation of the original work of creation. There was only one "creation." Consequently, Barth cautions that "to attribute the Church or revelation directly to creation or the creative will of God as such is to forget or ignore the fact that the Church or revelation can be an event only as an answer to the sin of man, or it is to be forced to try to integrate the sin of man into creation."[3] God has indeed accomplished more creations— salvation is "new creation"—but, for Barth, creation proper refers only to the first originating work.

As a work of God, Barth asserts that creation is also history. Creation was not a timeless act (as Augustine and those following him suppose); rather, as with salvation history, God took time as he created the world.[4] If creation were not history, Barth proposes, it would not be "the presupposition and preparation of the whole history which

1. Barth, *Church Dogmatics*, III/1, 117. Cf. 42 and 43. Hereafter I abbreviate references to Barth's *Church Dogmatics* with *CD* followed by the volume and part numbers and then the page number.

2. *CD* III/1, 215.

3. *CD* I/1, 446.

4. Langdon, *God the Eternal Contemporary*, 94–95.

follows it."[5] Accordingly, Barth interprets the seven days in the first Genesis creation narrative as part of creation history.

However, Barth also asserts that the creation history recorded in Genesis does not provide a precise account of *how* God created. Creation is not history as historians speak of it today. Rather, creation history is "non-historical history" or "pre-historical history." One reason for Barth's conclusion is that people were not there to observe the events of creation, so they could not record or verify what occurred. In addition, Barth finds that the Genesis accounts of creation are partially contradicted by references to creation elsewhere in the Bible.[6] He explains that the various biblical accounts of creation do have a common denominator and that the differences are found simply because the accounts were told for different purposes, by different sources. Given these factors, Barth does not interpret the creation narratives as literal history. At the same time, he insists that they are not "myth"—they are not a story teaching a timeless general principle, the characters of the story having the ability to be dispensed with. Rather, he describes the creation narratives as "sagas" expressing in poetic form the theological truth (i.e., actual event) that God created the world in history. In Barth's words, these sagas are "an intuitive and poetic picture of a pre-historical reality of history which is enacted once and for all within the confines of time and space."[7]

5. *CD* III/1, 77.
6. *CD* III/1, 80.
7. *CD* III/1, 81.

CREATION AS A DOCTRINE OF FAITH

Many people have supposed that the existence of creation and the act of creation can be understood apart from revelation. Barth, however, emphasizes that it is "*by faith* [that] we understand that the worlds were prepared by the word of God" (Heb 11:3, emphasis added).[8] As Barth works out the implications of his position, he argues that the doctrine of creation is a doctrine of faith, not a matter of natural theology. In other words, creation does not lead a person to faith; rather, faith leads a person to confess (and understand) creation.

Barth's intention is to present a Christian, and therefore truly theological (rather than philosophical or scientific) doctrine of creation. This, he believes, can only be done within the teaching of the church, and this understanding is indicated by the title of his major work, *Church Dogmatics*.[9] In practice, Barth insists that a Christian doctrine of creation is informed only by the revelation of Jesus Christ; in other words, knowledge of the world as creation has its noetic grounding in Christ. According to Barth, revelation in Christ is the basis for *all* of Christian theology (not only for this doctrine). Just as "God can be known only through God," creation also can only be known through God.[10] One cannot reason from nature to know that creation is created. Rather, in Jesus one learns that *God* is with *us*, the creation. Barth writes that "by becoming man in Jesus Christ, the fact has also become plain and credible that God is the Creator

8. *CD* III/1, 4 and 7.

9. According to Barth, "Dogmatics is the self-examination of the Christian Church" with regards to "the agreement of the Church proclamation done and to be done by man with revelation attested in Holy Scripture" (*CD* I/1, 11 then 248).

10. *CD* II/1, 79.

of the world. We have no alternative source of revelation."[11]
This means that knowledge of creation comes only by faith.
Barth's rejection of natural theology as a basis for the doctrine of creation is one of the unique (and controversial)
features of his doctrine of creation.

Content of the Article of Faith

According to Barth, the content of the doctrine of creation
requires that one place it in church dogmatics (which means
that the doctrine of creation must be grounded on the divine
self-witness). He offers three reasons why the doctrine of
creation *is not* other than an article of Christian faith[12] (that
is, belonging to church dogmatics), as well as an argument
for why it *is* an article of faith. First, the doctrine asserts an
actual existence of a reality distinct from God. In negative
terms, creation is not non-existing and God is not alone. In
contrast to Descartes' "I think, therefore I am," Barth posits
that this assertion is not self-evident and can be disputed.[13]
One might argue that life is just a dream. For Barth, such
self-doubts can only be replaced with certainty if the assertion of existence is based on the divine self-witness that
God has created. That is, our certainty is found in God, not
ourselves, because, for Barth, the reality of the creature is
what is in question, not the reality of the Creator.[14] Hence,
the divine self-witness is the only ground that can make
belief in creation something other than speculation or a
blind leap of faith.

11. Barth, *Dogmatics in Outline*, 43. Cf. *CD* IV/3, 149–50.

12. *CD* III/1, 5–22.

13. *CD* III/1, 350–63. Mangina, *Karl Barth*, 93.

14. *CD* III/1, 6; and Barth, *Dogmatics in Outline*, 43.

A second reason that Barth argues that the doctrine of creation is not other than an article of Christian faith is that it "asserts that this whole sphere [of creation] is *from God*, willed and established by Him."[15] This assertion includes the affirmations that God is the ground of the world's existence and that the world cannot be alone. These affirmations are, again, (Barth attests) not self-evident. Rather, one could just as well hypothesize that this is an eternal world or that there was a cosmic monster that created this world. All hypotheses following deductions from the human situation—for example, Schleiermacher's emphasis on a sense of absolute dependence—can be wrong and contradictory. Confessions of creation on these grounds are weak and uncertain. In contrast, Barth argues, doctrine properly flows from God to humanity, not from humanity to God.

Third, the doctrine of creation is not other than an article of Christian faith, Barth maintains, because the affirmation that God is the Creator of heaven and earth is determined entirely by the language and content found within Holy Scripture. The doctrine is therefore an appeal to faith and can only be accepted and known by faith. As is understood by the Christian affirmation of creation in the creeds, "God," who is the subject, "is not synonymous with the concept of a world-cause, rightly or wrongly postulated, disclosed or fulfilled."[16] Such a concept is, according to Barth, a product of human minds and belongs to the creaturely sphere. Rather, when speaking of "God," the church means specifically "God the Father of Jesus Christ." "Creator" includes a reference to a completed act of God, yet also to the one who is still involved with creation. It does not refer to a timeless relationship. Hence, Barth maintains that "it is for this very reason that the Creator cannot be

15. *CD* III/1, 7 (emphasis added).
16. *CD* III/1, 11.

changed into a world-cause, a supreme or first cause or a principle of being."[17] In contrast to the concepts of origination and causation (which are impersonal), creation refers to a divine action for which the only proper analogy is found within the life of God: the eternal generation of the Son. There is no parallel analogy found for creation within the life of creatures, for the act that the term "Creator" references cannot be compared with any other.[18] Furthermore, the objects of creation, "heaven and earth," refer to all reality that is distinct from God, both the visible and the invisible. Creation is more than just what man knows.[19] Nevertheless, ontologically heaven and earth are homogeneous; their "distinction is relative in view of their common distinction from God,"[20] who has created all things distinct from God, including matter and spirit. All of these concepts referred to in the doctrine of creation can, again, only be known through the self-positing of God.

Source of the Article of Faith

In addition to the above three reasons why the doctrine of creation *is not* other than an article of Christian faith, Barth offers an argument for why the doctrine *is* an article of faith: the doctrine is found true in the revelation of Jesus Christ.[21] When Barth says that we learn of creation in Christ, he means that the doctrine is found "in the perception, comprehension, understanding and estimation of the reality of the living person of Jesus Christ as attested

17. *CD* III/1, 13.
18. *CD* II/1, 76–77.
19. Barth, *Dogmatics in Outline*, 50 and 52.
20. *CD* III/1, 18.
21. *CD* III/1, 22–28; II/1, 515.

by Holy Scripture, in attentiveness to the range and significance of His existence, in openness to His self-disclosure, in consistency in following Him as is demanded."[22] It is not enough to just say that creation is the first thing the Bible teaches. Rather, creation is in the Bible to begin with because the whole Bible witnesses to Christ. And, Barth contends, when the Bible speaks of creation, it speaks of Christ. The christological basis of the doctrine of creation presents the doctrine "in such a way that the whole [of the church's confessional knowledge] necessarily stands or falls with the dogmas of creation as with every other constituent element."[23] In Jesus Christ one learns God became human and thus God is not alone, and also there truly is a reality distinct from God. Likewise, this union of God and the human indicates that people are not alone, because in Christ the church comes to know "God" as Christ's eternal Father.

When Barth argues that the doctrine of creation is solely an affirmation of faith, he highlights the noetic connections (i.e., Jesus as the revelation of creation) between Jesus Christ and creation. There are, however, also ontic connections (i.e., Jesus as the ontological ground of creation) because Jesus Christ, the divine incarnate Mediator, is the basis for the act and existence of creation. In fact, the noetic connection exists only because of this ontological connection. Barth comments, "Jesus Christ is the Word by which the knowledge of creation is mediated to us because He is the Word by which God has fulfilled creation and continually maintains and rules it."[24] Earlier theology, from Origen to the Reformers, noted the ontic relation but tended to neglect the noetic connection. Barth himself realizes

22. *CD* IV/3, 174.
23. *CD* III/1, 22.
24. *CD* III/1, 28.

that his emphasis on the noetic connection in Christ is a unique feature of his theology: "We emphasise something which has been strangely overlooked and neglected, or at any rate not developed in any detail, either in more recent or even in earlier theology."[25]

Position in *Church Dogmatics*

The placement of the doctrine of creation within *Church Dogmatics* also reveals something of Barth's belief that the doctrine of creation is an affirmation of faith. Barth places the doctrine of creation after the doctrines of revelation and God, which include his doctrine of election. John Godsey explains the reason for this deliberate placement:

> The Doctrine of Creation can properly come only *after* the Doctrine of God, the heart of which is God's Gracious Election. This structural arrangement signifies Professor Barth's conviction that God is not known first of all in His creation, but in the revelation of his Lordship in Jesus Christ. Only from the prior viewpoint of God's election or reconciliation, that is, only for the eyes of faith, does the world become a creation instead of a cosmos, does nature take on glory.[26]

Jesus Christ has accomplished salvation and in doing so is the revelation of God. It is through Christ, who is God, that we learn of creation, not the other way around. Accordingly, Barth affirms the being and existence of God before considering creation in depth. Therefore, the structural arrangement of *Church Dogmatics* further illustrates how

25. *CD* III/1, 29.

26. Godsey, "Architecture," 7 (original emphasis).

Barth views the doctrine of creation as an article of the Christian faith.

The Significance of Faith for the Doctrine of Creation

All of the arguments that we have been tracing indicate that Barth understood Jesus as the key to the "secret of creation"—that is, to the true knowledge of the existence and nature of the Creator and creation. This means that knowledge of creation, of the Creator and creature, is knowledge of faith. For Barth, faith is an attitude and decision. Faith "consists in the personal recognition that this reality is at the disposal of God as the theatre, instrument and object of His activity. It consists, therefore, in recognition of the fact that God has controlled and does and will control it. . . . [It is] a serious acceptance of God as Creator, a recognition of His right and power to control, a genuine reckoning with His control over past, present and future."[27] Faith is, therefore, to live in the presence of the Creator in recognition of God's power. As Barth notes, "those who believe in Jesus Christ have to do *ipso facto* with the Lord of heaven and earth."[28] That is, those who believe, encounter the Creator still. Here Barth identifies an analogy between divine action in the original creation and in the new creation: the Creator who says "Let light shine out of darkness" is the same one "who has shone in our hearts to give the light of the knowledge of the glory of God in the face of Jesus Christ" (2 Cor 4:6).[29]

Barth also describes faith as a recognition that all of creation belongs to God and will belong to God, and that

27. *CD* III/1, 32.
28. *CD* III/1, 35.
29. *CD* III/1, 33.

17

this ownership is not a matter of acquisition but of original possession. Accordingly, believers will submit to God and worship God. Furthermore, as the means by which believers live in the presence of the Creator, faith is also the means by which they recognize and experience God's benevolence. As Barth comments, "there has entered in in Jesus Christ the Bearer and Proclaimer of the benevolence of the One who willed and created the world and themselves."[30] In Christ we see that the Creator has always desired good for the creation, and since it is by faith that we recognize and experience the goodwill of this Creator, faith is central to the doctrine of creation.

Knowledge of creation is based in God's revelation in Jesus Christ. Hence, knowledge of creation starts with faith in God. Barth clearly does not want his doctrine of creation to be shaped by disciplines outside of dogmatics. Barth opens his doctrine of creation observing that "there can be no scientific problems, objections or aids" in understanding a Christian doctrine of creation.[31] On account of this statement and on account of Barth's position that the doctrine of creation is a doctrine of faith (revealed in Christ) rather than a piece of natural theology, some have concluded that Barth is completely opposed to any dialogue in regard to creation between theology and other disciplines, particularly the natural sciences.[32] Others, however, are less pessimistic and believe that Barth might have allowed for cosmology and theology to offer complementary accounts of creation.[33] One might suppose, for example, that Barth

30. *CD* III/1, 38.

31. *CD* III/1, ix.

32. Schwarz, *Creation*, 142; Cootsona, *God and the World*, 155; Aung, *Doctrine of Creation*, 261; Russell, *Cosmology*, 41; and Barbour, *Science Meets Religion*, 17–22.

33. Chung, "Karl Barth," 56–59; Mangina, *Karl Barth*, 90; Crisp,

would have allowed for a "faith seeking understanding" type of relationship between theology and science, where a study of science might provide some understanding of creation but without providing the condition for faith (nor the basis for this doctrine). In fact, on the page immediately following the apparent dismissal of scientific input quoted above, Barth expresses his openness to interdisciplinary dialogue when he writes that "future workers in the field of the Christian doctrine of creation will find many problems worth pondering" in the area of science and theology.[34] Overall, Barth refuses to ponder "scientific problems" because he wants to keep his doctrine of creation from being "contaminated" by non-theological sources during its formation.[35] However, Barth is certainly not of the opinion that nothing at all can be learned about creation outside of Jesus Christ.[36] Rather, throughout his doctrine of creation Barth is simply stating that one can only properly affirm and comprehend the knowledge of creation in light of the revelation of Jesus Christ.

One must remember that, for Barth, the doctrine of creation is not simply a statement *that* the world was created, but also (as noted above) a recognition of *who* the Creator is and what the relationship between this specific Creator and the creation implies; that is, the nature and meaning of creation. Natural theology cannot aspire to

"Karl Barth," 37; Fulljames, *God and Creation*, 17; and Webster, *Barth*, 111.

34. *CD* III/1, x. There might also be a basis for a theology-science interaction in Barth's theology of the created lights in *Church Dogmatics* IV/3. See Chung, "Karl Barth," 59; and Cootsona, *God and the World*, 150.

35. In Barth's rejection of natural theology he speaks of "a purifying of the Church" (*CD* II/1, 175).

36. See also his comments on the natural sciences and theological anthropology in *CD* III/2, 198–202.

these conclusions. Eberhard Busch rightly remarks that for Barth, in natural theology, "God is not only known via another *way*, but is known as *another* God: not the God who graciously links himself to humans but a God who, over against the world, exists abstractly *for himself*."[37] In addition, one must remember that, as Gregory Cootsona observes, "Barth's rejection of 'natural theology' derived not primarily from looking for God from the world as nature, but the world *as culture*."[38] In other words, Barth's rejection of natural theology was intertwined with his resistance to the Nazi regime and all those theologians who sought to justify the regime through their use of natural theology. This means that his resistance to natural theology cannot be equated with a resistance to science. He notes limits of science, but he does not present a precise definition of these limits.[39] Barth develops his doctrine excluding all sources outside of divine revelation in Christ, but other sources may be considered after the doctrine has been formed. His method does not hinder him from interacting with other disciplines, such as the natural sciences.[40]

37. Busch, *Great Passion*, 177 (original emphasis), cf. 69. Henry ("Karl Barth," 221) is no doubt correct to suggest that Barth is responding to Feuerbach's projection theory of religion, agreeing with Feuerbach that "any humanly projected God is indeed an idol." Cf. *CD* II/1, 80.

38. Cootsona, *God and the World*, 135. Also, Metzger, *Word of Christ*, 105 fn 88.

39. Moltmann, *God in Creation*, 36.

40. Consider the example of Torrance, *Space, Time and Incarnation*. Although he is a close follower of Barth, he nevertheless includes dialogue with science throughout his work.

Summary

In summary, Barth contends that the only certain doctrine of creation is the Christian doctrine of creation and that it is, thus, an article of faith. In other words, the doctrine of creation is not a piece of natural theology; it belongs in Christian dogmatics. Outside of Christian doctrine one can only speculate on the origin or purpose of creation and end in uncertainty. By contrast, within the Christian faith one meets Jesus Christ and learns of the "secret of creation"— the identity of the Creator and nature of creation. The revelation of salvation and creation belong together.[41]

THE CREATOR

The doctrine of creation, Barth notes, is first of all a doctrine of the Creator. After all, the creed "does not speak of the world, nor even, I believe in the work of creation. But it says, I believe in God the Creator. . . . Fundamentally what is involved here is the knowledge of the Creator."[42] For Barth, the doctrine of creation speaks of two criteria of true deity: freedom and love. In his criteria, one finds a reaffirmation of Barth's doctrine of the divine perfections (traditionally, "attributes"). Indeed, Barth affirms once again in *CD* III/1 his central thesis from his doctrine of the divine perfections (*CD* II/1) that "God is the One who loves in freedom."[43] According to Barth, God is "the One who loves" in the sense that God seeks to create fellowship. God "wills and completes this fellowship in Himself" eternally and also "wills

---

41. *CD* III/1, 414.

42. Barth, *Dogmatics in Outline*, 41, cf. 42.

43. *CD* III/1, 50, and *passim*. Cf. *CD* II/1, 257, and *passim*.

as God to be for us and with us who are not God."[44] God is free in that God's act is God's own as God loves. Hence, divine freedom consists not only in the absence of limits and restrictions (which theologians often emphasize with reference to the aseity or transcendence of God); rather, divine freedom also consists in God's freedom to determine to be in fellowship—to love.[45] Therefore, love and freedom are not opposites. In God's love, God is free and in God's freedom, God loves.[46] This aspect of Barth's doctrine of God comes through again in his doctrine of creation as the work of creation is a divine work of freedom that is grounded in love.

The Freedom of the Creator

Barth affirms that creation has come about as a result of the free will of God: "It is the divine will and accomplishment in relation to man—and nothing else—which really stands as the beginning of all things."[47] This is foundational for his doctrine of creation for it is a statement about the aseity and freedom of God and implies that everything that exists, other than God, is dependent upon God for its existence.[48] God was free to create. It was not an emanation of his being that he could not control, nor was creation necessary. There was nothing intrinsic, nor extrinsic, that made creation necessary. It was God, and God alone, who determined to create. Barth bases this insight, of course, on Jesus Christ:

44. *CD* II/1, 275 then 274.

45. *CD* II/1, 301–4.

46. *CD* II/1, 322.

47. *CD* III/1, 99.

48. Barth equates the freedom of God with divine aseity in *CD* II/1, 202.

"In that God became man, it has also become manifest and worthy of belief that He does not wish to exist for Himself only and therefore to be alone."[49]

As far as intrinsic necessity is concerned, Barth argues that God has no need of creation, or humans specifically (as part of creation). God is complete in Godself and is self-sufficient: "God has no need of us, He has no need of the world and heaven and earth at all. He is rich in Himself. He has fullness of life; all glory, all beauty, all goodness and holiness reside in Him. He is sufficient unto Himself, He is God, blessed in Himself."[50] Since God experiences love within the eternal divine life *ad intra*, God already has relationality within Godself and does not need a creation to relate to.[51] If God had not created there would still have been no lack in God. This does not mean, however, that God cannot relate with creation. In fact, God's freedom allows God to do just this.[52]

With regards to extrinsic necessity, God did not require the cooperation of anything—not another agent or reality—to create. Barth emphasizes here the difference between the church dogma of creation and the creation doctrines of other ancient religions where the origin of the world was portrayed with images of sexual processes, spitting, or struggle.[53] In contrast to such portrayals of creation,

49. Barth, *Dogmatics in Outline*, 41.

50. Ibid., 44–45. Cf. *CD* III/1, 7.

51. *CD* II/1, 499.

52. Deegan, "Christological Determinant," 122, notes how some criticize the concept of aseity for portraying God as so independent and disconnected from the world that God is unable to relate to it, but that Barth overcomes this concern.

53. *CD* III/1, 112, 243 and *passim*.

the divine will and nothing else "stands at the beginning of all things."[54]

By asserting that creation was the will of God, Barth identifies creation as having a personal origin. As noted above, the concept "Creator" cannot be equated with any "first cause." Rather, the Creator is God, who interacts with creation in the covenant of grace.[55] The Creator has a goal or direction for creation. More specifically, Barth identifies the work of creation with the will of God the Father: "It is as this Eternal Father [of Jesus Christ], determined in the act of His free expression and therefore not from without but from within, determining Himself in His Son by the Holy Spirit and Himself positing everything else, that He is also the Creator."[56]

The fact that the original creation is a result of the will of God is further illustrated by the fact that God completed the work. That is, God was in control and was able to stop the act of creation. Barth recognizes this in God's rest on the seventh day of creation in the Genesis creation narrative: "it is precisely this rest which distinguished God from a world-principle self-developing and self-evolving in infinite sequence."[57] God was free to limit his creative activity.

The Love of the Creator

Barth also affirms that creation is grounded in the eternal love of God, and that therefore God's will is not arbitrary.[58]

54. *CD* III/1, 99.

55. *CD* III/1, 44.

56. *CD* III/1, 11, cf. 50.

57. *CD* III/1, 215. Cf. III/3, 7.

58. Where Berkouwer (*Triumph of Grace*) and Aung (*Doctrine of Creation*, 38–41) have preferred to speak of the grace of God in Barth's doctrine of creation, I have, following Barth's emphasis,

This grounding is especially important for the doctrine of creation because the freedom of God demands that God has no need of a creation. Consequently Barth asks, "how can there be something alongside God, of which He has no need? This is the riddle of creation."[59] In answer Barth insists that God has always had loving intentions toward creation, and that the Creator's love is seen in God's grace toward humans. For example, God graciously keeps chaos from overtaking humanity (Gen 1:6–8) and provides for all of humanity's needs in creation.[60]

By affirming the love of God in creation, Barth draws together the works of creation and salvation. "God does not have two loves," as Iain Torrance states,[61] but rather, Barth observes, the same God who is the Creator is also the Savior. God loves creation in respect of his Son who was to assume human nature because "Jesus Christ stood eternally before Him as the Elected and Resurrected."[62] From this point of view, one may say that Jesus Christ is the basis of God's love for creation and that, therefore, "His being and activity *ad extra* is merely an overflowing of His inward activity and being, of the inward vitality which He has in Himself."[63]

According to Barth, although creation is not eternal, it was eternally the object of God's love. By "eternal" Barth means that it was always God's intention to create. Barth

---

preferred the concept of love. Grace focuses on the merit (or rather, the *lack* of merit) of the receiver. In contrast, love focuses on the action and attitude of the giver, here the Creator. It is because of the love of the Creator that the Creator is gracious. Love is the ground of grace.

59. Barth, *Dogmatics in Outline*, 45.

60. *CD* III/1, 134.

61. Torrance, "Trinity in Relation to Creation," 37.

62. *CD* III/1, 51; and II/2, 104.

63. *CD* II/2, 175.

speaks of God loving "man and man's whole world from all eternity, even before it was created."[64] The problem with affirming this view of God's love is that it seems to imply that God's act of creation was necessary. In this respect, Colin Gunton asks of Barth, "if God loves the creature from eternity, is he not in effect bound to create it?"[65] Indeed, Barth even affirms that God created "under no other inward constraint than that of the freedom of His love."[66] Nevertheless, it is crucial to remember that creation proceeds not only from the love of God, but also from the will of God. Accordingly, Barth is also able to speak of God's "eternal decision regarding creaturely history."[67] God was free to choose to create. Creation comes, then, from the *freedom* of His love. When keeping both aspects in mind one can see that the affirmation of the love of God harmonizes with the above affirmation of God's will. Barth expresses it this way: God "wants in His freedom actually not to be without man but *with* him and in the same freedom not against him but *for* him, and that apart from or even counter to what man deserves. He wants in fact to be man's partner, his almighty and compassionate Savior."[68] God, in his freedom, wills to love humanity, God's creature. In Barth's words, "God is the One who loves in freedom."[69]

---

64. *CD* III/1, 50.

65. Gunton, *Triune Creator*, 163. Likewise, Metzger, *Word of Christ*, 109.

66. *CD* III/1, 15, cf. 51.

67. *CD* III/1, 15.

68. Barth, *Humanity of God*, 50.

69. *CD* II/1, 257; III/1, 50, and *passim*.

Creation out of Nothing

From the outset of his doctrine of creation Barth affirms that God created out of nothing (*ex nihilo*).[70] Barth maintains that "Creator means: *creator ex nihilo*."[71] Historically the doctrine of *creatio ex nihilo* is a primary way that theologians have affirmed that creation is exclusively the result of the will of God. Barth, however, takes a uniquely christological approach to the doctrine as he presents the doctrine primarily in light of the love of God as expressed in the resurrection. In Barth's approach to the doctrine of *creatio ex nihilo*, he combines an emphasis on both divine freedom and love and, thereby, again affirms that God is the basis of all that is distinct from God.

In affirming the doctrine of *creatio ex nihilo* Barth begins with affirmations that are typical of the historic formulations of this doctrine in the church.[72] He explains that creation out of nothing means, first, that creation was not out of some pre-existent non-being thing that was brought into being. Second, creation was not formed from pre-existent material since there was no reality that existed eternally other than God. Third, God knew creation before he created it. God's ideas shaped and preceded his creation, but the ideas were not something existing externally to God. Fourth, although God uses materials in creation, for example, to create humans, this is not divine emanation but the use of materials that were created out of nothing. Last, the doctrine means that there was no possibility of things being created or existing outside of God's creative activity. All of these affirmations are important because, as Barth notes, they oppose the heresies of emanation (monism)

70. *CD* III/1, 4.

71. *CD* II/1, 76.

72. *CD* III/1, 108.

and an eternal co-existent with God (dualism). Rather, all creation derives from God's will and love.

As Barth explores the basis for the doctrine of creation out of nothing, he is inconsistent when he considers Old Testament passages that refer to creation. First he notes the unique use of *bara'* (created) in Genesis 1:1, stating that it "is lexicographically unequivocal" and that it "can denote only the divine creation in contrast to all other: the creation which does not work on an existing object or material which can be made by the Creator into something else; the *creatio ex nihilo* whose Subject can only be God and no one apart from Him—no creature."[73] The conflicting interpretation comes later in the same volume where Barth, being more conservative in his interpretation, writes, "it may well be that the concept of a *creatio ex nihilo, of which there is no actual hint in Gen. 1–2*, is the construct of later attempts at more precise formulation. But its antithesis—the mythological acceptance of a primeval reality independent of God—is excluded in practice by the general tenor of the passage as well as its position within the biblical context."[74]

Despite this particular inconsistency, Barth otherwise is consistent and clear in his position that *creatio ex nihilo* is a christological insight. He draws a parallel between creation and resurrection (though he also recognizes that creation does not require pre-existing matter while resurrection does). Furthermore, he argues that the New Testament took this parallel for granted (cf. Rom 4:17; Heb 11:3). Just as God is the one who calls humanity into a new life at the resurrection, God is the one who calls humanity, and all of creation, into existence at creation. Expressing this parallel, Barth writes that "as creation is *creatio ex nihilo,*

73. *CD* III/1, 16.

74. *CD* III/1, 103 (emphasis added).

so reconciliation is the raising of the dead. As we owe life to God the Creator, so we owe eternal life to God the Reconciler."[75]

Barth draws five insights from *creatio ex nihilo* in light of its connection to the resurrection. While one might reach these conclusions apart from reflecting on the resurrection, he finds that the resurrection is a proper basis for these affirmations. First, Barth argues that the resurrection-creation connection implies that humanity is given direction: "As there stands behind it [humanity] God and His Word, it is not *ex nihilo* but very much *ex aliquo* [from somewhere]."[76] That is, as God (specifically) awakens humanity with resurrection life, humanity is not found in an absurd or meaningless world of random chance. Second, Barth emphasizes that it is not the void, nothingness, or chaos that is the origin of humanity, but rather that it is God. Third, the Son of God, who is the prototype of humanity, provides a pre-existence for humanity. Fourth, humanity's "being summoned includes and therefore has as a presupposition his [*sic*] constitution, his existence as a natural and spiritual being."[77] Nevertheless, the actual form of humanity has no presupposition and is not shaped by this presupposed summons. Last, the only possibility of the existence of humanity comes from God, whom humanity can stand before only by faith.

Behind all of these points stands Barth's insight that faith is believing for things not seen, things which God brings into existence. In the New Testament this includes creation and the resurrection. Although this insight is only stated explicitly in the context of a discussion of humanity (i.e., resurrection), and accordingly points only to the

75. *CD* I/1, 413. Cf. III/2, 152–53.

76. *CD* III/2, 155.

77. *CD* III/2, 155–56.

creation of humanity, Barth clearly extends the implications to the whole of creation.[78]

Barth concludes his discussion of creation out of nothing by reemphasizing the significance of the New Testament parallel between creation and resurrection. He writes, "the theology of the ancient Church failed to base the doctrine of the *creatio ex nihilo* on this biblical insight. . . . Once it is understood in this light, it is no mere theologoumenon, but what it is intended to be in Heb. 11:3 and unquestionably in the context of Heb. 11 and Rom. 4, namely, an article of faith which is necessary in its own place."[79]

Summary

Barth's doctrine of creation presents God the Creator as the one who freely and lovingly created. Nothing forced God to create. God alone stands behind creation, which means that creation is made with purpose. That creation has purpose is reflected further in the doctrine of creation out of nothing where Barth highlights that God summons the creature into existence just as God summons in resurrection.

CREATION AND COVENANT

Aside from discussing the Creator, one of the key questions asked in a doctrine of creation is "why is there a creation?" For Barth the answer is the covenant—the commitment and act of God to be in relationship with humanity; a

---

78. For example, Barth uses it to defeat dualism and monism and makes such statements as, "the doctrine of the *creatio ex nihilo* makes the same affirmation of all creatures . . ." (*CD* III/2, 156) Cf. I/1, 413.

79. *CD* III/2, 157.

commitment fulfilled in Jesus Christ.[80] If Barth's doctrine of creation is prized for anything, it is its uniting together of the doctrines of creation and reconciliation. In regards to the significance of this aspect of Barth's doctrine of creation, Jonathan Wilson comments, "the integrity of creation and redemption in Christ was recognized, asserted, and defended throughout the early church and the Middle Ages. Only in modernity has this integrity been largely abandoned and forgotten."[81] However, Wilson continues, Barth stands out as a bright spot in modernity in his presentation of the unity of the covenant and creation.

This unity is the center of Barth's doctrine of creation. As seen above, Barth recognized that the identity of the Creator is also the Savior. The doctrine of the Trinity leads Barth to unite the two works of creation and reconciliation.[82] When he turns to expound the Genesis creation narratives, he writes that "they do not speak of the work of any creator of the world, but—like all that follows—of words and acts of the very One who later made Himself known and attached Himself to the people of Israel as *Yahweh-Elohim*."[83] Ultimately, it is the same God who saves that creates. In fact, Barth argues that the ground and goal of creation is the covenant. This is expressed in his theses that creation is the external basis of the covenant and the covenant is the internal basis of creation.

80. I explore the meaning of covenant in more detail in the latter part of chapter 5.

81. Wilson, *God's Good World,* 50.

82. *CD* III/1, 50, 64.

83. *CD* III/1, 65.

Creation Allows for Actualization of the Covenant

When Barth argues that creation is the external basis of the covenant, he means that creation allows for the actualization of the covenant. There must be a creation, and at the center of that creation, humanity, the covenant partner, in order for there to be a covenant. Election of humanity to the covenant presupposes or includes what one could call the election of creation to existence. There must be an arena for and an object of God's love. While creation is not the ground or cause of the covenant, it is implied or presupposed by the covenant, and Barth maintains that "in the purpose of creation as such we are concerned only with the making possible and not the actualisation of this other divine work."[84] In this sense creation is the "technical possibility" for, the "stage" for, or the "way" to the covenant. Creation is not the covenant, but leads to it. The goal of creation is the covenant and thus creation is, to some extent, a means to an end. God creates a covenant partner, in humanity, and humans need the remainder of creation as their home and to provide for their needs.[85]

However, creation is more than simply a means to an end because it also points forward to the covenant. As Hans Urs von Balthasar observes, for Barth, "the nature of creation is its preparation for grace."[86] In Barth's words, creation is the "equipment for grace."[87] He also speaks of "a prophetical view of creation," by which he means that creation is preparation for and aiming immediately at

<hr>

84. *CD* III/1, 47.

85. Chapter 3 discusses how this causes Barth's doctrine of creation to have an anthropocentric character.

86. Balthasar, *Theology of Karl Barth*, 111. Cf. *CD* III/1, 97.

87. *CD* III/1, 231.

covenant history.[88] Given that creation leads to grace in the covenant, creation itself may be considered grace. Indeed, the grace of the covenant is prefigured in creation.

Barth finds his thesis that "creation is the external basis of the covenant" reflected in Genesis 1:1—2:4a.[89] In this passage God creates the world by God's Word but does not allow chaos to exist. Rather, God rejects this possibility and leads creation to grace. Furthermore, God's mercy does not allow the primal floodwaters to threaten creation nor the sea to flood the dry earth, and all that opposes God and God's salvation is overcome. God then provides food for humans by creating plants and trees even before humans existed to ensure the continuance of humanity. The creation of animals before humans serves as a sign that the earth is safe to live in. Therefore, Barth proposes, "creation means peace—peace between the Creator and creatures, and peace among creatures themselves."[90]

The external basis of the covenant (creation) is finally reached with the creation of humanity. Humans are created in the image of God. Barth suggests that this should be interpreted only in a relational fashion as he argues that the image of God is found in differentiation and relationship. Barth presents an analogy of relations: as God is uniquely and originally a relational being, humans are made relational beings. This is exemplified in male and female relationships. At the same time, Barth cautions that "the differentiation and relationship between the I and the Thou in the divine being, in the sphere of the *Elohim*, are not identical with the differentiation and relationship between male and female."[91] That is, sexuality and individuality pertain to creatures. However,

88. *CD* III/1, 233 and 231.

89. *CD* III/1, 98–228.

90. *CD* III/1, 209.

91. *CD* III/1, 196.

God created and wills a being capable of being God's and its own (*viz.* other humans) counterpart. Humans are free for relationship with other humans and for relationship with God (but only as God is for them). Upon the creation of humanity, then, creation is ready for the covenant.

Upon the seventh day of creation God rests and, as noted above, this rest illustrates that creation is complete and ready for the covenant. Indeed, Barth asks whether God could "have rested if He had not done all these things with a view to Christ."[92] God knows the future and God's rest is justified and explained in view of Jesus Christ as the form of the creature, as it is to this rest that God invites humanity in the covenant. On account of this, Barth claims that creation is the external basis of the covenant.

Covenant as the Impulse for Creation

Barth's second major thesis—that the covenant is the internal basis of creation—means that the covenant is the impulse, reason, or goal of creation.[93] Oliver Crisp challenges Barth, proposing that God's self-glorification (i.e., the glory of God) is the goal of creation, rather than covenant.[94] However, this is not an either-or situation. While God does create for God's glory, God is indeed glorified through the covenant. As Barth writes, "*the covenant* between God and man *is the meaning and the glory*, the ground and goal of heaven and earth and the whole creation."[95]

92. *CD* III/1, 222, quoting H. F. Kohlbrügge.

93. *CD* III/1, 228–329.

94. Crisp, "Karl Barth," 30–31 and 42–43. Mangina (*Karl Barth*, 88) rightly notes that giving "glory" as an answer to why God created, lacks concreteness.

95. Barth, *Dogmatics in Outline*, 50 (emphasis added). Cf. *CD* III/1, 213.

Furthermore, Barth's claim that the covenant is the internal basis of creation does not contradict the idea that creation is the "external" basis of the covenant, but rather qualifies it. Covenant is not an implication of creation, but is that which is the ground of the existence of creation. God wills the covenant and therefore he creates. Hence, the covenant exists before creation and is not just an afterthought. As Barth states, "Before the world was, before heaven and earth were, the resolve or decree of God exists in view of this event in which God willed to hold communion with man."[96] This means that creation has meaning and purpose.

Creation comes from the same free love that desired the covenant and creation must be viewed "not as an accident but as a sign and witness of this necessity."[97] Hence, Barth refers to the idea that the covenant is the internal basis of creation as the sacramental view of creation.[98] By this he means that creation reflects the covenant that is its ground. Creation is a sign of the covenant because it is shaped according to this purpose and goal. Therefore, according to Barth,

> what God has created was not just any reality—
> however perfect or wonderful—but that which
> is intrinsically determined as the exponent of
> His glory and for the corresponding service.
> What God created when He created the world
> and man was not just any place, but that which
> was foreordained for the establishment and the
> history of the covenant. . . . The fact that the
> covenant is the goal of creation is not some-
> thing which is added later to the reality of the
> creature, as though the history of creation might

96. Barth, *Dogmatics in Outline*, 54.

97. *CD* III/1, 229.

98. *CD* III/1, 233.

> equally have been succeeded by any other history. It already characterises creation itself and as such, and therefore the being and existence of the creature. The covenant whose history had still to commence was the covenant which, as the goal appointed for creation and the creature, made creation necessary and possible, and determined and limited the creature.[99]

In other words, "If creation takes precedence historically, the covenant does so in substance."[100]

Barth finds his thesis that the covenant is the internal basis of creation reflected in Genesis 2:4b–25, which is a saga independent from 1:1—2:4a. In this creation narrative, God is referred to specifically as Yahweh Elohim, the God of the covenant who saves and reveals the divine name to Israel. As Barth interprets the second creation narrative, it reflects not the general beginning of the world but rather the creation of the people of Israel. In creation, God makes humans living souls, "a soul quickened and established and sustained by God in a direct and personal and special encounter of His breath with this frame of dust."[101] God is the one who gives life and is able to take it away, the full implication of which comes in light of the fall of humans and the subsequent confirmation of God's faithfulness to humanity when God continues, despite the lapse, to give life. Here, Barth suggests, a covenant between God and humanity is present already in creation: "The second creation saga embraces both the history of creation and that of the covenant, both the establishment of the law of God and the revelation of His mercy, both the foundation of the world and that of Israel, both man as such and man elected and

99. *CD* III/1, 231.
100. *CD* III/1, 232.
101. *CD* III/1, 237.

called. This is the theological explanation of its peculiarity." Yet it does this without confusing the two elements of creation and covenant. It "understands creation in the light of the covenant."[102]

Barth also finds his thesis that the covenant is the internal basis of creation emphasized in the biblical portrayal of the Garden of Eden. In this story, God made man and then placed him ("woman" has not yet entered the story) in the garden. It was not necessary for God to do so, yet God created humanity for this special place. This place is not humanity's possession, however, but God's. Nevertheless, God uses it as a sanctuary for humanity. In this respect, Barth views the garden as analogous to Israel and the promised land of Canaan. Furthermore, a river originates in this garden, which miraculously divides to cover the whole earth. This represents the divine favor, of which humanity gets to partake first. There are also two trees in the garden. The tree of life serves as a sign that people may truly live, for God is with them and has given them rest. It serves a role analogous to the tabernacle in the life of Israel. The second tree, the tree of the knowledge of good and evil, is only a sign of a possibility. It is not the tree of death, but it points to this possibility because only the Creator can bear this knowledge. Humans will necessarily be crushed under this weight (and indeed Israel does suffer). However, it is not a snare for humans because humans are only free to accept the direction of God, not to reject God. As Barth explains, "if the creature could on its own judgment reject what on God's judgment it ought to accept, it would be like God, Creator as well as creatures."[103] Each tree says—one positively, one negatively—that one should live by the will of God. The freedom humans have is "the sign of the fellowship already

102. *CD* III/1, 240.
103. *CD* III/1, 258.

established between God and man at his creation."[104] As this whole story is analogous to the salvation history of Israel, Barth notes that this story presents salvation history as the meaning of creation: covenant is the internal basis of creation. Barth also suggests that these passages truly point to Jesus Christ, who fulfills the freedom given to humans and confirms the election of humanity to fellowship.

The creation of woman, says Barth, also displays that the covenant is the internal basis of creation.[105] It was not good for man to be alone, and in this second narrative the emphasis is on the woman being brought to man to fulfill his need. The resulting marriage relationship completes the creation of humans and corresponds to and prefigures the covenant, as the relationship is analogous to the covenant of God with Israel and also to that of Jesus Christ with the church. Overall, Barth's thesis that the covenant is the internal basis of creation expresses that God creates because of the covenant.

Summary

At the center of Barth's doctrine of creation is his twofold thesis that creation is the external basis of the covenant and covenant is the internal basis of creation. In this Barth indicates that creation is necessary for the covenant to take place and that the covenant is the reason that God creates.

ADDITIONAL INSIGHTS AND EMPHASES

No less important than all of Barth's emphases highlighted so far in this chapter, Barth also affirms throughout his

104. *CD* III/1, 265.
105. *CD* III/1, 288–329.

doctrine of creation (and elsewhere) that creation is distinct from God and that creation is good. Barth views creation as distinct primarily in light of its relationship to the Creator. It is a relationship of freedom and dependence. Likewise, Barth identifies creation as good in light of the relationship between the Creator and the creation: Creation is good because the benevolent God is its Creator and creates with purpose and direction.

Creation as Distinct from God

While some question whether Barth can logically affirm the Creator/creation distinction (see chapter 5), Barth does consistently affirm the historic Christian belief that creation is distinct from God. The distinction is part of his definition of creation for he reasons that an emanation from God "would really not be creation, but a living movement of God, an expression of Himself. But creation means something different; it means a reality distinct from God."[106] Barth recognizes the Creator/creation distinction primarily in the incarnation of Jesus Christ, the God-man. However, it is also recognized, even confirmed, from other viewpoints.

For Barth, the concept of covenant implies the distinct nature of creation. That is, the covenant presupposes a relationship between distinct beings as only a being distinct from God could be a real covenant partner.[107] For both God and creatures, this is a relationship of freedom: the Creator is free to be in relationship with the creature and, subsequently, the creature has freedom to be in relationship with the Creator. This affirmation of the freedom of the Creator

106. Barth, *Dogmatics in Outline*, 46.
107. *CD* III/1, 184.

(see earlier) further confirms that creation is distinct from God, for a creation that is a result of God's free will excludes pantheistic and panentheistic systems.[108] In Barth's view, the relationship between the Creator and creation and the distinction between them exist not only at the time of creation but also continues eschatologically into the future:

> And as [creation] it did not proceed from God's own being, but was freely created by God, so it cannot return to God, nor can it or should it in any way forfeit or surrender its autonomy in face of Him. God is to be all in all (1 Cor 15:28), but this does not really mean that the "all" will no longer be, that God will be alone again. It means rather that in the final revelation of His ways He will be seen by the creature to have attained His ultimate goal in all things with the creature, the creature not ceasing to be distinct from Himself.[109]

This relationship of distinction is also seen in God's current presence in the world. Indeed, Barth points out that for God to be omnipresent means God is present to something other than God.[110]

Barth's emphasis on the dependent character of creation also expresses the Creator/creation distinction.[111] One might be tempted to say that creation is "contingent," but such a term seems impersonal, like "cause." This is probably one reason Barth himself avoided the term "contingent." In addition, while contingency connotes the uncertainty and non-necessity of an occurrence, dependence speaks of the

108. *CD* II/1, 562.

109. *CD* III/1, 86. On this point see Jenson, "Creator and Creature," 219–21.

110. *CD* II/1, 462–63.

111. *CD* III/1, 207 and 344.

actual relationship between the Creator and creation. And creation is dependent upon the grace of God for its existence and sustenance. Barth argues that examples like God's impartation of breath to creatures, which is necessary for their existence, exemplify this, just as the tree of life within the Garden of Eden also symbolizes dependence.[112]

Barth's use of analogy further confirms the dependence of creation and therefore the Creator/creation distinction. The divine work of creation is analogous to the Father's eternal generation of the Son. In addition, humans, made in the image of God, are analogous to God's relationality. These analogies are limited, however, so they should not be taken as equations between God and creation. Rather, even they in themselves imply a distinction between God and creation; for example, there is no analogy within creation for the act of creation.[113] This is an act distinct to the Creator. Furthermore, Barth rejects the concept of an *analogia entis* (analogy of being), or at least certain interpretations of it.[114] His primary concern is to insist that God and creation are not in the same category of "being." Thus, God is hidden and cannot be known until God reveals Godself.[115]

In fact, Barth's analogies themselves are based, or dependent, upon God and not creation. They only work in one direction. Aung rightly observes that "this similarity consists in the fact that what is common to them [God and

112. *CD* III/1, 282–83 and 382.

113. *CD* II/1, 76.

114. *CD* I/1, xiii, 166; II/1, 83–84; III/2, 220; Barth, *Holy Spirit*, 5. While Balthasar (*Theology of Karl Barth*, 163–64, 382) and others have suggested that Barth eventually changed his mind about the *analogia entis*, Johnson (*Karl Barth and the* Analogia Entis, 158–230) persuasively argues that Barth continued to reject the *analogia entis* throughout his career. Cf. McCormack, "Karl Barth's Version of an 'Analogy of Being,'" 88–144.

115. *CD* I/1, 320.

creation] exists primarily and properly in the first one, and then in the second because the second is dependent upon the first."[116] Therefore, Barth's proposition that all theological analogies start with God also confirms that God is distinct from creation.

Barth's understanding of ethics also displays the Creator/creature distinction. In his view, ethics particularly belongs within church dogmatics because it follows the command of God.[117] This belief becomes evident in his doctrine of creation as he discusses the tree of the knowledge of good and evil. To Barth, the tree signifies that humans are to live by the will of God, who properly possesses the knowledge of good and evil.[118] In contrast, humans cannot bear the weight of this knowledge and were not meant to. Barth insists that "unlike God's, man's decision will be a decision for evil, destruction and death: not because he is man, but because he is only man and not God."[119] For Barth, creatures are distinct from God in that they have differing abilities and roles from God with respect to ethics.

Barth also clearly affirms the Creator/creature distinction through his explanation of the demythologization of creation in the Genesis creation narratives. For example, in his exposition of Genesis 1 he notes that the reason light is not identified with the luminaries is in order to correct those who believe in astral deities. Unlike in other ancient creation myths, in the Genesis narrative the luminaries are given the demythologized and subservient role of merely marking time. Likewise, the self-perpetuating life of

116. Aung, *Doctrine of Creation*, 63.

117. *CD* I/1, xiv. Webster (*Barth's Ethics*) argues that ethics is central to Barth's *Church Dogmatics*.

118. *CD* III/1, 257–58.

119. *CD* III/1, 261.

vegetation (God says "bring forth") demythologizes the deity of earth.[120] By rejecting the deity of creation in his interpretation of these texts, Barth further illustrates his belief in the Creator/creation distinction.

Lastly, for Barth creation is also distinct from God with regards to time. Creation is confined to time. Time is the living space of creatures and God is not limited to it.[121] Further, Barth maintains that time, or more precisely, created time, had a beginning, and while he generally does not speak of it as a creation of God, he does affirm that time began with God's creation.[122] In fact, creation is a historical work in time and created time began, according to Barth, with "the Word of God which summoned light and called and made it day."[123] This time is necessary for history—time being the sphere of history—and history is necessary for the covenant.[124] Created time is, however, distinct from God's time, which is eternity. While it is not the case that eternity is the antithesis of created time, as eternity is not timelessness but pure duration, the chief characteristic of created time is that it is a one-way sequence.[125] On the other hand, God's "time," or eternal "time," is the immediate unity of past, present, and future. God is before time, over time, and after time—pre-temporality, supra-temporality, and post-temporality. This distinction between created time and God's time is a further confirmation of Barth's belief in the Creator/creation distinction.

120. Whitehouse, "Karl Barth," 49–50.

121. *CD* III/1, 130. Langdon, *God the Eternal Contemporary*, 85–122.

122. *CD* III/1, 15, 42, 60, 68; and Barth, *Dogmatics in Outline*, 46.

123. *CD* III/1, 129.

124. *CD* III/1, 72.

125. *CD* III/1, 67; III/2, 519; II/1, 608–77; and Barth, *Dogmatics in Outline*, 46–47.

Goodness of Creation

Given that the covenant is the internal basis of creation and that the covenant entails redemption, one might wonder if creation is good. That is, given its basis, it might seem that creation is in need of redemption from the very start and, therefore, not good.[126] Barth, however, goes to significant lengths to affirm, with the Christian tradition, that creation is good. He begins by emphasizing that creation's existence is not neutral—it does not "just" exist. Nor is it ungodly or anti-godly; God saw creation and said that it was good. However, its goodness is not something that is intrinsic to it, but rather, it is good because the Creator identifies it as such. This creation is the creation that God wanted. Hence, Barth maintains, "God does not grudge the existence of the reality distinct from Himself."[127]

Creation is good not just in the fact that it is, but that it has a goal. Creation's goodness is teleological.[128] And its goal is, as we have seen, the covenant. According to Barth, "what God has created was not just any reality—however perfect and wonderful—but that which is intrinsically determined as the exponent of His glory and for the corresponding service."[129] The Creator has made creation suitable for the covenant and directs creation towards it; therefore, creation is good.

Creation is good because creation is the result of God's "Yes." God does not create that which he rejects (nothingness) and therefore creation corresponds with his will. Creation is also limited in this sense: Barth writes that "this

126. Metzger, *Word of Christ*, 108–9; and Busch, *Great Passion*, 176.

127. Barth, *Dogmatics in Outline*, 45.

128. *CD* III/1, 413, 215, 245; and III/3, 42.

129. *CD* III/1, 213.

whole realm that we term evil—death, sin, the Devil and hell—is *not* God's creation, but rather what was excluded by God's creation, that to which God has said 'No.'"[130] Similarly, Barth observes that God calls the light, which he creates, "good," but not the darkness, which is simply the antithesis of light.[131] The forces of evil are, however, not beyond God's rule and control. Barth is not teaching dualism because evil forces are not another god with which God must contend.

Creation is also good in the sense that it is a good work of God. Barth develops the idea that "creation is benefit."[132] In Herbert Hartwell's words, creation is "divine blessing."[133] The goodness of creation is no mere assertion. It is good because it originates with the Creator, who only creates that which is good. This is God's nature and to neglect this is to neglect that the Creator is also the Savior. For Barth, all of God's works are united in the covenant. By contrast, if one separates creation from the covenant then one is pressed to conclude, with Marcion, that creation is evil. The identity of the Creator and his divine benevolence distinguishes the Christian doctrine of creation from all other concepts of creation, be they mythical, religious, or philosophical, because the Christian doctrine of creation presents a unique origin and course for creation and, therefore, affirms that creation is good.

If God affirms creation as good, then it must follow, Barth reasons, that creation has been actualized.[134] The work of creation brings the creature into existence and

130. Barth, *Dogmatics in Outline*, 48 (original emphasis); and *CD* II/1, 560. On creation, sin, and nothingness see Krötke, *Sin and Nothingness*, 35–48.

131. *CD* III/1, 120.

132. *CD* III/1, 330–414.

133. Hartwell, *Theology of Karl Barth*, 118.

134. *CD* III/1, 213 and 344–65.

sets the creature into its own mode of existence, which is determined by its Creator. By actualizing the creature God has brought Godself into relationship with it. God creates a sphere to love and act in and on. Barth writes, "to be a creation means to be determined to this end, to be affirmed, elected and accepted by God."[135] God commits himself to creation. This is the meaning of the covenant, and thus creation, being actualized for this purpose, is good.

For Barth, that creation is good also implies that its existence is justified.[136] It is Jesus Christ who justifies creation, for he fulfills the covenant. God says "Yes" and accepts creation in Jesus Christ. We see God's "Yes" being confirmed in the brighter side of creation (though not proven by it), that is, all that would conventionally be labeled "good"— the joys of life. In other words, creation's "yes" confirms the Creator's "Yes."

At the same time, the revelation in Jesus Christ confirms the shadow side of creation (which is a mark of creaturely finitude, not necessarily evil) because it reveals that creation is being liberated from an actual darker side of creation. Nevertheless, this darker side is absolutely transcended. In saying "Yes" God is defeating the shadow side, even though God's "Yes" includes his "No." In Barth's words, "It can be seen at once that there can be no question here of an end in itself. The No is not said for the sake of the No but for the sake of the Yes. We cannot stop at the suffering death and burial of Jesus Christ. This is not a final word."[137] The existence of this darker side does not disqualify the justification of creation, for Jesus Christ's "action, His own participation in light and darkness, life and death, implies

135. CD III/1, 364; and II/1, 117.

136. CD III/1, 366–414.

137. CD III/1, 384.

either way the justification of creation."[138] Furthermore, the fulfillment of the covenant shows that creation is perfect, that is, perfect for the covenant. It is the best creation because it is the creation made according to the will and plan of God. God created a creation that was in need and capable of being exalted to covenant relationship. In this sense even the shadow side or imperfection of creation is part of its perfection, and the fact that God overcomes our imperfection justifies creation. God's "Yes" is ultimate and creation begins with and aims at this "Yes." Even its future glorification adds nothing to the perfection of creation because, Barth attests, its glorification "presupposes that it is already perfectly justified by the mere fact of its creation."[139]

Barth is not advocating philosophical optimism. Rather, "divine revelation manifests both the sorrow and joy of life, and therefore not only permits but commands us to laugh and weep."[140] Consequently, a Christian doctrine of creation differs from optimism because it focuses on Jesus Christ. As Barth attests,

> the meaning and truth of Christian optimism consist in His [Jesus Christ's] lowliness and exaltation, in His death and resurrection as the secret of the divine will in creation and the divine good-pleasure in the created world. It is the fulfilment of the covenant in Him which shows us that the two opposites of life both have their necessity and seriousness since they are both grounded in an eternal dimension.[141]

138. *CD* III/1, 383.

139. *CD* III/1, 366.

140. *CD* III/1, 375.

141. *CD* III/1, 412–13. Cf. Berkouwer, *Triumph of Grace*, 65–69; Meynell, *Grace versus Nature*, 90.

By focusing on Jesus Christ, Christian "optimism" does not eliminate but assimilates the shadow side of creation. It affirms that creation has an imperfection.[142] Hence, unlike optimism, it does not base its positive judgment on the world. In Barth's mind, such a judgment has no authority and wrongly supposes a goodness intrinsic to creation; by contrast, Christian optimism regarding the goodness of creation is based on a recognition of the Yes of the Creator as revealed in Jesus Christ.

Summary

Throughout his doctrine of creation, Barth makes clear that creation is distinct from God and that creation is good. He recognizes this Creator/creation distinction primarily in Jesus Christ. His affirmation of the Creator/creation distinction is confirmed by his insistence that there is a true covenant partner outside of God, that the covenant relationship is one in which creation is dependent upon God, by his understanding of ethics, his demythologization of creation, and by his understanding that God is not limited to created time. Barth recognizes that creation is good on account of the fact that creation is created and directed by the benevolent Creator toward the covenant. God creates the good creation just as God desires it to be, including both its imperfections and joys. Both of these emphases—the Creator/creation distinction and the goodness of creation—are made in light of the covenant relationship between the Creator and creation.

142. Therefore, as with Irenaeus, Barth does not see creation as originally in a state of perfection. Berkhof, *Christian Faith*, 167; and Gunton, *Triune Creator*, 55–56 and 164.

CONCLUSION

Barth's doctrine of creation expands on what it means to say that creation was by, for, and in Christ. As a work of God, creation is revealed in Christ. The doctrine of creation is, therefore, an article of faith. Barth insists that the "secret of creation"—the identity and nature of the Creator and creation—can only properly be known as certain on account of the revelation of God in Jesus Christ. This doctrine teaches not only the existence of creation, but also about the Creator who creates in freedom and love. These teachings are expressed in Barth's central theses that creation is the external basis of the covenant and that the covenant is the internal basis of creation. Since God creates for covenant and because of the covenant, it is clear that creation is distinct from its Creator and also that creation is good. Having highlighted the primary emphases in Barth's doctrine of creation, I turn now to bring further clarity to his doctrine of creation by evaluating how various interpreters have critiqued his presentation of this doctrine.

3

Searching for a Theology of Nature

The most common critique of Barth's doctrine of creation concerns its anthropocentric character.[1] Such critiques usually begin with the observation that Barth focuses on humanity to the neglect of nature, that is, all of non-human creation. The result of this neglect, many claim, is that Barth cannot address contemporary issues regarding nature, such as ecological concerns. Although this concern is justified in part, Barth does not completely neglect nature. Wolf Krötke is certainly correct in his assessment that

---

1. Moltmann, *History and the Triune God*, 128; Webster, *Barth*, 112; Tanner, "Creation and Providence," 125; Santmire, *Travail of Nature*, 146–55; Torrance, *Karl Barth*, 132; Sherman, *Shift to Modernity*, 229–36; Young, *Creator, Creation and Faith*, 100–102; McLean, "Creation and Anthropology," 115; Watson, *God and the Creature*, 167; Barbour, *When Science Meets Religion*, 22; Whitehouse, *Creation, Science, and Theology*, 15; and Fulljames, *God and Creation*, 57.

"the heart of Barth's doctrine of creation is anthropology,"[2] nevertheless it is also the case that Barth's doctrine offers insights that may contribute to a theology of nature. To illustrate this, I proceed by first outlining the various facets of Barth's doctrine of creation that have led to the anthropocentric critique, and then turn to consider insights found within Barth's doctrine of creation that show that he has not completely neglected nature. Finally, I respond to a number of theologians who have proposed corrections to the anthropocentrism within Barth's doctrine of creation.

ANTHROPOCENTRIC ELEMENTS

The road to anthropocentrism begins with Barth's central thesis that creation is the external basis of the covenant and the covenant is the internal basis of creation. Salai Aung finds that in Barth's explication of this thesis "creation is subordinated to the idea of covenant both structurally and conceptually."[3] With respect to the structure of Barth's doctrine, his statement that creation is the external basis of the covenant takes precedence over the statement that the covenant is the internal basis of creation. This imbalance is evident in his introductory and concluding chapters in *Church Dogmatics* III/1, both of which stress the external statement and its emphasis on the goal of covenant over creation. In regards to the conceptual subordination of creation, many interpret Barth's position that creation is the external basis of the covenant (which Barth emphasizes structurally) as implying that creation is not an end in itself, but only a means to an end. Accordingly, Colin Gunton and Paul Metzger characterize Barth's fault more

---

2. Krötke, *Sin and Nothingness*, 45.

3. Aung, *Doctrine of Creation*, 274.

as a subordination of creation to redemption rather than as anthropocentrism.[4] Even so, Gunton argues that this subordination remains detrimental to the status of the whole of the material world in Barth's theology. In Barth's explication of his thesis that "creation is the external basis of the covenant," he portrays creation as simply the stage on which the covenant is played out or as the vehicle to the covenant. That is, nature often appears to be nothing more than the arena for the object of God's love, but not itself an object of God's love. For example, Barth writes that creation is "the presupposition of the realization of the divine purpose of love in relation to the creature."[5] Here Barth clearly subordinates creation to the covenant and portrays creation as a means to an end.

A second area in which Barth's doctrine of creation is anthropocentric is in his exposition of the Genesis creation narratives. These sections take up the majority of *CD* III/1, and in them all of creation is interpreted with regards to its use for humans.[6] Accordingly, heavenly bodies, while not divine, are recognized as useful for people by marking time. Further, God is understood to graciously prepare a table for humans before they are created, and humanity is considered the crown of creation. Barth concludes his analysis of this passage of Scripture with the assertion that "creation ended with man, having found its climax and meaning

4. Gunton, *Triune Creator*, 165; and Metzger, *Word of Christ*, 119. From an alternative perspective, Cootsona (*God and the World*, 154) writes, "it could be argued that redemption subsumes creation in Barth's dogmatics. I would rather underline the greater gain that Barth has strongly *related* God and the world through his close connection of redemption and creation" (original emphasis).

5. *CD* III/1, 96.

6. Meynell, *Grace versus Nature*, 82; and Fulljames, *God and Creation*, 58.

in the actualization of man."[7] In response, Syd Hielema observes that Barth here "diminishes the significance of the creation and thereby diminishes the role of the internal statement in the doctrine of creation."[8] Hence, this second critique reinforces the first critique noted above.

Barth's christological focus is a third cause of Barth's anthropocentrism in his doctrine of creation.[9] For Barth, knowledge of creation is found chiefly in Jesus Christ. That is, in Jesus Christ one learns that God became human, and thus, that God is not alone, and that there truly is a reality distinct from God. Barth writes that "by becoming man in Jesus Christ, the fact has also become plain and credible that God is the Creator of the world. We have no alternative source of revelation."[10] Additionally, Barth presents Jesus Christ as the beginning and the goal of creation as Christ fulfills the covenant.[11] In response to this christological focus, Norman Young carries the criticism of anthropocentrism further than most others and concludes that Barth's theology actually discourages theological attention to non-human creation. He reasons that if knowledge of creation begins and ends with Jesus Christ, theological interest is immediately limited to the relationship between God and humans. This focus on Christ brings a methodological constraint to Barth. Young finds this to be true of Barth's earlier and later theology. In his earlier theology, Barth focused on the gap between the Creator and creatures, while in his later theology he focused on God overcoming this gap. However, the overcoming of this gap is explained almost completely

7. *CD* III/1, 213.

8. Hielema, "Disconnected Wires," 81.

9. Tanner, "Creation and Providence," 125; and Watson, *God and the Creature*, 167.

10. Barth, *Dogmatics in Outline*, 43. Compare *CD* IV/3, 149–50.

11. *CD* III/1, 42, 90, 232, 396. Compare *CD* II/1, 667.

in human terms. Young laments that "in the *Dogmatics* Barth posited an act of God's grace that preceded the creation, namely the election of Jesus Christ before time and us in him. By giving priority in this way to the election of humanity rather than to the creation of the world Barth has actually increased the emphasis on man, and the rest of the created order becomes even more dependent and derivative than before."[12]

On the one hand, Young expresses his disappointment that Barth's theology does not and cannot give theological direction to the current ecological crisis. On the other hand, Young concludes his discussion on an encouraging note, claiming that Barth's approach does not necessarily leave one with nothing to say regarding the ecological crisis, nor does it necessarily encourage the exploitation of creation. In fact, Barth's theology, in particular his theology of the fall, leads one to appreciate the scope of the problem and realize that the change necessary in people to reverse the crisis can only come as a result of the grace of the Creator. Nevertheless, the fact remains that Barth's christological focus leads him to an anthropocentric doctrine of creation.

Fourth, Barth's doctrine of creation is anthropocentric because he presents humanity as the only creature who is a partner in the covenant.[13] Indeed, Barth often uses the word "creature" when referring to humanity alone.[14] Furthermore, Barth maintains that "he [man] alone is honored to be God's partner in the covenant of grace" and that "the covenant is God's encounter with man with a view to being

12. Young, *Creator, Creation and Faith*, 101.

13. Moltmann, *History and the Triune God*, 128; Hielema, "Disconnected Wires," 88; and Aung, *Doctrine of Creation*, 74.

14. For example, *CD* III/1, 59, 97, 110, 230, 345, 363, 377, and 382.

man's salvation in His own person."[15] Accordingly, when Barth speaks of the work of creation in the context of the covenant he is concerned primarily with the existence of human beings. In one place he even defines creation anthropocentrically as "the divine establishment of human existence as such."[16] When considered in relation to Barth's statement that creation is the external basis of the covenant, the above quotation suggests that for him it is primarily human beings that are the external basis of the covenant. This further illustrates Barth's anthropocentric doctrine of creation.

Fifth, anthropocentrism arises in Barth's doctrine of creation on account of his anthropocentric doctrine of election. Balthasar correctly observes that election is "the heartbeat of his whole theology."[17] Hence, Barth's doctrine of election is foundational for his doctrine of creation and his "covenant" thesis. In fact, he defines covenant as the election of grace.[18] It is unquestionable, then, that for Barth election and covenant are inseparable. We even find him using the terms almost interchangeably. Consider the following passage:

> The eternal decree of God which precedes creation and makes it possible and necessary is the gracious *election* of man in Jesus Christ. And God's *covenant* of grace with man, in which God makes Himself Lord and Pledge and Saviour of His people and therefore the God of all men, is the internal basis of creation. It is not, then, the case that God first determined Himself as

15. *CD* III/1, 178, then IV/2, 760.

16. *CD* III/1, 281.

17. Balthasar, *Theology of Karl Barth*, 174. Cf. McCormack, *Karl Barth's Critically Realistic Dialectical Theology*, 460–63.

18. *CD* II/2, 9.

> Creator, then made man His creature, and only
> then in a later development and decision *elected*
> man and instituted His *covenant* with him. On
> the contrary, it is for the sake of this *election* and
> in relation to this institution that He created
> heaven and earth and man.[19]

These phrases with respect to election bare a strong resemblance to Barth's creation/covenant thesis: similar to how he expresses that "the covenant is the internal basis of creation," Barth says "for the sake of this election" God creates and that election "precedes creation and makes it possible." Barth comes near to saying that "election" (rather than the covenant) is the internal basis of creation. This is not unexpected as Barth asserts that all God's works are "grounded and determined in the fact that God is the God of the eternal election of His grace."[20] The problem from the perspective of the current discussion is that Barth understands election as an election of only humanity in Jesus Christ. The whole of creation is not elect. Rather, creation is only the external basis of the election, or the covenant. It is clear, then, that the relation of the covenant (and thus creation) and election also leads Barth's doctrine of creation to be anthropocentric.

Barth's anthropocentrism appears not to be accidental. H. Paul Santmire quotes Barth as saying in conversation, "What . . . did that [nature] have to do with the faith of the Holy Bible?"[21] Furthermore, within the *Church Dogmatics* Barth writes that "the attempt to penetrate to the inner secrets of the relation between God and the rest of creation [i.e., non-human creation], and the consequent attempt to explain and present the latter from the standpoint of this

19. *CD* III/4, 39–40 (emphasis added).

20. *CD* II/2, 14.

21. Santmire, *Nature Reborn*, 117.

relation, can never be more than exercises in pious surmise or imagination."[22] Such an attitude and posture hindered Barth from dwelling on nature to any great extent.

BEYOND ANTHROPOCENTRISM

Nevertheless, Barth certainly does not suggest that a relationship between God and nature does not exist. Nor does Barth totally neglect nature in his writing. "Anthropocentrism" denotes a focus and neglect, but the neglect is not necessarily complete. Among those of Barth's insights that concern creation as a whole, there are four significant points at which he transcends his own anthropocentrism. First of all, Barth is clear that *all* of creation has its origin in God. This includes nature. Furthermore, Barth acknowledges that upon the completion of creation, God declared that the whole of it was good (in the sense that this is the creation that God wanted and that it is directed toward the covenant).[23]

Second, and in relation to the critique that Barth presents humanity as the only creature who is a partner in the covenant, Barth also acknowledges that nature participates in the covenant. That is, covenant does in some way embrace the whole of created reality. Nature is not only the home of humanity, but, Barth submits, it also participates in the covenant through humanity. However, how it does this is a mystery. He proposes that "it is only in this relationship, in dependent connection with man, that the animal kingdom can and will participate in the mystery of all creation as it is revealed in man, and in the promise of this mystery. The ascription of this position and function to man does

22. *CD* III/2, 17.

23. *CD* III/1, 212–13 and 366. On this point, see the latter section of chapter 2 in this book.

not mean that the rest of creation is excluded from this mystery; it describes the manner of its inclusion."[24] Barth's awareness that all of creation participates in the covenant is evident in his description of the future redemption and perfection of the world, which includes the new heaven and the new earth.[25]

In light of Barth's emphasis on the place of humanity in the covenant it is almost surprising to see how he speaks of covenant at times. Barth observes that even before the creation of human beings "in God's blessing of the fish and birds we really transcend the concept of creation and enter the sphere of God's dealings with His creation. What we have here is the beginning of its history, or at least an introductory prologue which announces the theme of this history, i.e., the *establishment of a covenant* between God and His creation." Barth presents God's blessing of animals "as an element in the history of creation but already as an element in the history of the covenant."[26] Furthermore, he speaks of God's history with Abraham as most properly revealing and executing—not commencing—"God's covenant with the earth."[27] Such assertions not only run counter to Barth's typical emphasis on humanity in the covenant, but also counters his suggestion that creation only participates in the covenant through humanity. In contrast to Jürgen

24. *CD* III/1, 187. See *CD* III/1, 178 and 223. Compare Tanner, "Creation and Providence," 125–26, who notes that for Barth the covenantal "privilege of human beings does not exclude other creatures from having their end in Christ; it merely specifies the manner of their inclusion. As Israel mediated participation in fellowship with God to the nations, so humanity has its hope in Christ in indissoluble connection with the hope of the whole cosmos." See also Heilema, "Disconnected Wires," 91.

25. For example, *CD* III/1, 17, 18, 149, and 237.

26. *CD* III/1, 170 (emphasis added).

27. *CD* III/1, 151.

Moltmann's interpretation of Barth, Barth does not relate "God's covenant to human beings and only to them,"[28] but, rather, he recognizes that all of creation participates in the covenant. An important consequence of this recognition is that Barth does not view creation exclusively as a means to an end. It is still this (in as much as creation is the external basis of the covenant). However, insofar as the covenant is the goal of creation, creation participates in that goal. This insight into creation's participation in the covenant also, then, softens the first and fourth critiques noted above, which state that in Barth's doctrine of creation humanity is the only creature who is a partner in the covenant and that Barth subordinates creation to the idea of covenant.

Third, Barth notes the ordered nature of creation. Hielema praises Barth for this insight, even though it does not take the prominent position he believes that it should be given. He complains that Barth is over-anxious about natural theology in his doctrine of creation and that this obscures some of his theology, causing some of his finest points to be missed. Hence, Hielema emphasizes Barth's "joyfully free affirmation of the creation characterized by ordered creatureliness within a context that denigrates this same creation."[29] "Ordered creatureliness" means living in right relationship. This includes human relationships with God, and within this relationship, human relationships with nature as well. Furthermore, within these relationships creatures are interdependent and, moreover, all dependent upon the Creator. Thus, Barth notes that with

28. Moltmann, *History and the Triune God*, 128.

29. Hielema "Disconnected Wires," 89. This idea of "ordered creatureliness" differs from a concept of the "order(s) of creation," a concept that Barth generally does not wish to endorse in the *Church Dogmatics* (even though he does employ the term in a qualified sense at times). See Nimmo, "Orders of Creation," 29 (esp. fn 29).

respect to creatures, "Man is not their Creator; hence he cannot be their absolute lord, a second God."[30] For Barth, human lordship is finite. This insight clearly has ecological implications. Humans have finite lordship and are not creators to do as they please with creation.

Fourth, although Barth emphasizes the utility of creation for humans throughout his exposition of the Genesis creation narratives (see the second critique above), within his exegesis of Genesis 2, Barth observes that humanity has a responsibility to the rest of creation. He draws on Genesis 2:5, which states that "no plant of the field was yet in the earth and no herb of the field had yet sprung up" in part because "there was no one to till the ground." In this context, Barth notes, God creates humanity to be gardeners. As gardeners, people are "destined . . . to serve the earth." And in service to creation, humanity fulfills the meaning of their existence. They are "to till and keep the earth." In this action, humanity "is responsible to both God and the creature."[31] While these affirmations of Barth are enough to support a theology of creation care, Barth continues by adding that through their service to creation, humanity serves as a sign that God will eventually fulfill the hope of creation by bringing it to perfection.[32]

SUGGESTED CORRECTIONS

There are, then, at least four ways in which Barth moves beyond his own anthropocentrism in his doctrine of creation. At the same time, a number of theologians have suggested ways to correct Barth and move further beyond

30. *CD* III/1, 187. On this point, see Sherman, *Shift to Modernity*, 232.

31. *CD* III/1, 237. Cf. 251 and 254.

32. *CD* III/1, 237–38.

the anthropocentrism that does, nevertheless, exist in his doctrine.

In relation to the critiques of Barth's doctrine of creation that observe that this doctrine is based on an anthropocentric doctrine of election and that humanity is the only creature who is a partner in the covenant for Barth, Aung suggests that Barth's tendency to subordinate nature could be corrected by viewing creation as a whole as God's covenant partner.[33] Similarly, Santmire wonders whether it would "be possible, in a Barthian mode, to think of God electing nature, as well as humanity, in Christ."[34] Hence, he also wonders if nature could then be viewed as a "covenant partner" with God. Can all of creation be considered a covenant partner? From a Barthian perspective, the answer must be *no*. How could inanimate objects, such as rocks, be partners in anything? This does not seem possible. According to Barth humans are God's covenant partners because, as Kathryn Tanner observes, they "knowingly and freely respond."[35] While one might suppose that animals could be covenant partners with God in this respect, it is difficult to see how this covenant relationship could apply to the whole of creation.[36] Further, although one could qualify the above suggestion by positing that creation should be viewed as *participating* in the covenant, that is, by reaping its benefits, this would not be an improvement on Barth, for as we have seen, he has already made this assertion.

Moltmann also suggests corrections for Barth's doctrine of creation. First, he suggests that all of creation

33. Aung, *Doctrine of Creation*, 277; Cf. Fulljames, *God and Creation*, 58; and Gunton, *Triune Creator*, 180.

34. Santmire, *Travail of Nature*, 171–72.

35. Tanner, "Creation and Providence," 125.

36. Similarly, Barth notes that in creation vegetation did not need blessing, only living creatures (*CD* III/1, 174).

participates in the covenant. As noted above, Barth affirms this. Second, Moltmann proposes that the ground and goal of creation is not covenant, but rather the future kingdom of glory.[37] Moltmann feels that it is necessary to be eschatologically oriented and focus on the end goal of creation, with creation being interpreted in terms of its direction and process towards liberation. Accordingly, nature is not neglected because God will be all in all in the kingdom of glory.

However, Moltmann's advance is not an advance at all. First, his eschatological emphasis denigrates the significance of all that comes between creation and the eschaton, that is, salvation history. Secondly, and most importantly, his suggestion presupposes that the covenant ends at the beginning of the kingdom of glory. This is also implied in Moltmann's statement that "at the end of the history of the covenant stands not the covenant . . . but creation again: the new creation."[38] In actuality, Barth's emphasis on the covenant embraces and corrects Moltmann's suggestions. Where the work of *creation* clearly ends according to Barth, there is no suggestion that the *covenant* ends with the new creation. In fact, one even finds hints that the covenant is only fully realized in the new creation. Barth writes that the realization of the covenant "can only be the work of His [God's] incomprehensible mercy, and how it can only be an event through the passing and renewal of man *and of the world*."[39] He also speaks of the Creator's activity as directing history towards reconciliation *and redemption* and maintains that the covenant is fulfilled in Jesus' death

37. Moltmann, *God in Creation*, 4–5, 55–56; and Moltmann, *History and the Triune God*, 128–30.

38. Moltmann, *History and the Triune God*, 129.

39. *CD* III/1, 275 (emphasis added).

and resurrection.[40] Covenant includes the way to the kingdom of glory as well as the kingdom itself. Indeed, it is only
in the kingdom of glory that the covenant is fully realized
and God is God, and people are God's people. In Barth, the
complete historical covenant is recognized as significant.

It is clear that "anthropocentrism" in Barth's doctrine
of creation must not be understood to mean a complete
neglect of nature. Indeed, for Barth the whole of creation
participates in the covenant. Barth does not develop a
theology of nature; nevertheless, this does not inherently
mean that something within his theology needs correction.
Rather, in neglecting nature Barth has simply not said all
that can be said.[41] In light of the present need to reflect
theologically on nature given the environmental crisis,
Barth's basic approach to understanding creation does not
so much need to be corrected as extended or supplemented.
For example, his christological approach might be supplemented by a pneumatological approach to the doctrine of

40. *CD* III/1, 75 and 115. Granted, Barth makes a distinction
between the covenant and the kingdom, writing that "the covenant
is the promise of the kingdom. The kingdom is the fulfillment of
the covenant" (*CD* IV/2, 760). However, this is not an absolute distinction given that he views the kingdom as the fulfillment of the
covenant and on account of the fact that he includes the idea of
"kingdom" within "covenant" in the above given passages (Cf. *CD*
III/1, 46). Also, Barth attests that creation is made to be the theatre
of God's glory (*Dogmatics in Outline*, 49) and that "the primal and
basic purpose of this God in relation to the world is to impart and
reveal Himself—and with Himself His glory, He Himself being the
very essence of glory" (*CD* II/2, 140). He also speaks of redemption
and eternity being the goal and end of all creation in the same way
he speaks of the covenant (*CD* II/1, 629). Compare this conclusion
with Balthasar (*Theology of Karl Barth*, 108) who takes Barth's understanding of the covenant to mean "the incarnation and redemption."

41. Similarly, although Barth recognizes the creation and existence of the invisible world (i.e., heaven), he does not dwell on it to
any great extent.

creation, which has indeed proven to be fruitful for many theologians.[42] Such an approach would overcome the limitations of Barth's christological focus (with its resulting anthropocentrism) by highlighting, among other points, the presence of God through all of creation as the Spirit renews the face of the earth (Ps 104:30) in anticipation of the day when the Spirit will liberate creation "from its bondage to decay" (Rom 8:21).

CONCLUSION

Barth's critics are correct to label his doctrine of creation anthropocentric. His christocentrism, his presentation of non-human creation as a means to an end, and his focus on the God/human relationship in the covenant hinders him from developing a sustained theological discussion of nature. Barth does not, however, completely neglect nature. He asserts that the whole of creation is that which God wanted, and is therefore good, and that all of creation participates in the covenant. He also describes a creation that is ordered toward right relationships, including relationships with nature, and he views humanity as gardeners who are responsible to serve the earth. Some have suggested ways that Barth's understanding of the covenant should be revised so as to move beyond his anthropocentrism, but his concept appears to be superior. He understands that the covenant includes God's loving and free relationship and lordship over the whole of his creation—after all, God is also God of nature—even though Barth emphasizes God's relationship with humanity. Having discerned these insights in Barth's doctrine of creation, one may incorporate them into

42. Consider, for example, Moltmann, *God in Creation*; Johnson, *Women, Earth, and Creator Spirit*; Gunton, "Spirit Moved," 190–204; and Gabriel, "Pneumatological Perspectives," 195–212.

a theology of nature that would supplement Barth's insights by emphasizing the participation of the whole of creation in the covenant and its being liberated by the Spirit from bondage to decay. The fact that Barth's doctrine of creation might be supplemented pneumatologically causes one to wonder whether or not Barth is adequately Trinitarian in his doctrine of creation. The following chapter will address whether or not this is the case.

4

Trinity and Creation

In seeking to articulate a Trinitarian doctrine of creation, it might seem profitable to turn to Barth's doctrine of creation for insight given that he is often credited with reviving Trinitarian theology, including within his doctrine of creation specifically.[1] However, one might refrain from turning to his doctrine of creation for Trinitarian insights too quickly, given that some theologians have questioned how successful he was in employing the doctrine of the Trinity in this aspect of his theology. On the one hand, Herbert Hartwell has written that in Barth's doctrine of creation, creation is "intrinsically trinitarian in its ontology."[2] On the other hand, Thomas F. Torrance concludes that Barth did

1. Jenson, "Karl Barth," 47, and Gunton, *Triune Creator*, 157.
2. Hartwell, *Theology of Karl Barth*, 114. Cf. Crisp, "Karl Barth on Creation," 28–29.

not develop his doctrine of creation "from an overarching *Trinitarian* perspective."[3]

Theologians who are critical of Barth's Trinitarian approach, or lack thereof, in his doctrine of creation, critique him for offering a seemingly twofold interpretation of the image of God, for presenting God as outside creation, for a modalistic understanding of God's relation to the world, and for a binary understanding of divine creativity. Most of these critiques arise from misunderstandings of Barth. Nevertheless, while Barth certainly affirms that the identity of the Creator is the triune God, there is a binary character in his understanding of divine creativity in that he has little to say regarding the activity of the Holy Spirit in the work of creation.

INCONSISTENTLY TRINITARIAN?

Image of God

One critique concerning Barth's doctrine of creation concerns his Trinitarian explanation of the image of God. Following a rejection of an analogy of being (*anologia entis*) between God and humanity, Barth argues that the image of God is not a matter of being but of relation. That is, in contrast to those who have argued that the image of God consists of a quality in each person, Barth argues that the image of God is relational, consisting of one's relationship with God and with other people. Reflecting on Genesis 1:26–27, Barth follows early Christian exegesis and posits that the divine "*let us* make humankind" (v. 26) is grounded in God's self-differentiation within the life of the Trinity. Grounded in divine relationality, the image of God is, then, expressed not in the creation of some aspect of an individual

3. Torrance, "Interaction with Karl Barth," 61.

human being. Rather, the image of God comes as God creates people in relationship. It is "them" who God creates in the image of God—"male and female he created them" (v. 27).[4] Besides the textual considerations and the support of early Christian exegesis, Barth is here interpreting the creation of human beings in the light of the covenant. Man is given a covenant partner in woman to remind him of the covenant with God. As Hugo Meynell observes, for Barth the man-woman relation "is one of the clearest illustrations of the internal basis of creation in the covenant which is the very reason for its existence."[5]

Salai Hla Aung argues that Barth is inconsistent in his application of the Trinitarian approach to understanding the image of God. He determines that Barth was correct to interpret the image of God in a social sense, but that he erred by interpreting the image of God in a twofold fashion as an I-Thou relationship. He interprets Barth to mean that "humans [were] created after the model of the Trinity" and, therefore, Aung contends that a truly Trinitarian understanding of the image of God must be threefold.[6] Accordingly, Aung builds on Elizabeth Frykberg's critique of Barth by interpreting the Trinitarian image of God in a threefold fashion as an I-Thou-He/It relationship, with the third aspect of the image being a child.[7] He suggests that this threefold interpretation is concordant with concrete human relationships.

4. *CD* III/1, 183–86 and 191–96.

5. Meynell, *Grace versus Nature*, 86.

6. In contrast, Old Testament scholars tend to be critical of Barth for interpreting the *image of God* in a Trinitarian sense at all. See MacDonald, "*Imago Dei* and Election," 305 and 311.

7. Aung, *Doctrine of Creation*, 34–35, 268, and 274. Cf. Frykberg, *Karl Barth's Theological Anthropology*, 42–46 and 50–52.

Aung's proposed correction to Barth's understanding of the image of God seems arbitrary, or, at best, a product of natural theology.[8] The latter seems evident in his appeal to concrete human relationships as a foundation for his proposal. In his I-Thou-He/It proposal, there seems to be nothing that would keep someone from adding another fourth aspect (other than the fact that God is *tri*une) or (more likely) from supplying something else in place of the relation to the child. So, for example, in liberation theology one might wish to place a relation across cultural or racial boundaries into the image of God. Thus the model would be I-Thou-Other Culture. There is no dogmatic reason for preferring Aung's proposal of referring to the image of God in a threefold manner by adding a "child" as the third aspect of the image of God instead of adding an alternative third aspect to one's understanding of the image of God.

Beyond the somewhat arbitrary nature of Aung's proposal, a more significant problem with his proposed correction of Barth's interpretation of the image of God is that he incorrectly concludes that Barth is interpreting the image of God in a twofold fashion, exclusively in terms of male/female relationships.[9] For Barth, the image of God is based only on an *analogy* of relations that runs as follows: as the triune God is uniquely and originally relational being, humans are made relational beings. Hence, the image of God is found in differentiation and relationship. Barth highlights an example of this in male-female relationships.

8. One might argue that Barth is himself engaging in natural theology in his use of "I-Thou" language, which he borrows from the existentialism of Martin Buber, but it seems that Barth uses this language more as a means of expressing the relationality of the image of God as revealed in Christ, rather than using the concept of "I-Thou" as a means of building up a doctrine of the image of God on the basis of natural theology.

9. Aung, *Doctrine of Creation*, 268.

However, all analogies point to discontinuity. Accordingly, Barth points out that there is no sexuality in God. Likewise, the divine persons are not *individuals* like humans given that humans do not have the same perichoretic unity found among the divine persons. As long as one remembers the limits of analogy, one can recognize that Barth is not presenting a twofold interpretation of the image of God. Focus should not be placed on the number three (given the *tri*-unity of God) nor on a dual sexuality since Barth does not claim that the image of God is expressed only in a relationship between two people, but rather simply that it is expressed in relationship. The analogy is of "free differentiation and relation."[10] Rather than searching for a threefold interpretation of the image of God, it is important to understand that Barth correctly recognizes the relational aspect of the image of God (even though one may critique Barth for understanding the image of God exclusively in relational terms).[11]

Sphere of God

A second reason that theologians sometimes critique Barth for being inconsistently Trinitarian in his doctrine of creation is because they believe Barth presents God as being in a different sphere from the world. H. Paul Santmire, for example, argues that according to Barth God's immanence in the created world is limited to heaven, that is "in the realm of the spiritual, with the angels, not on earth."[12] Similarly,

10. *CD* III/1, 185. Cf. Price, *Karl Barth's Anthropology*, 161; Frykberg, *Karl Barth's Theological Anthropology*, 32; and MacDonald, "*Imago Dei* and Election," 315 and 322.

11. Gabriel, "Trinitarian Doctrine of Creation," 38–39.

12. Santmire, *Travail of Nature*, 154. Cf. Young, *Creator, Creation and Faith*, 84; and Aung, *Doctrine of Creation*, 270–71.

Peter Fulljames recommends supplementing Barth with additional pneumatological reflections "in order to clarify how God is distinct from the world yet is intimately related to all things at all times."[13]

The criticism that Barth presents God as outside the sphere of creation illustrates a misunderstanding of Barth. Barth indeed speaks of God as "outside" creation and as having a "divine space" distinct from "creaturely space."[14] However, these affirmations are made first of all in a metaphorical or ontological sense rather than a spatial sense; that is, in order to say that creation is distinct from God and God exists without creation before God creates. Similarly, Vladimir Lossky notes (with a quotation from St. John of Damascus), creation "is of another nature than God. It exists outside of God, 'not by place but by nature.'"[15]

At the same time, Barth argues that God does possess space and even that God's space is always in created space.[16] Most importantly for Barth, God's close relation with our created sphere is indicated by the fact that "God is with us" in Jesus Christ. For example, he writes that "in Jesus Christ there is no isolation of man from God or of God from man."[17] As a result, even though Barth speaks of God's place being heaven, he concludes that "so surely is something done on earth as subsequently and from heaven that it too becomes the place of God."[18] Furthermore, when Barth discusses God's omnipresence he speaks of our space

13. Fulljames, *God and Creation*, 129, cf. 89. I discuss Barth's understanding of the role of the Holy Spirit in creation below.

14. For example, Barth, *Dogmatics in Outline*, 43–46; and *CD* I/1, 142; II/1, 536; III/1, 25, 43, 70–71, 97, 349; and III/3, 436ff.

15. Lossky, *Orthodox Theology*, 51.

16. *CD* II/1, 476.

17. Barth, *Humanity of God*, 46.

18. *CD* III/3, 444.

existing within God's space, God surrounding creation, and even creation existing in God.[19] Barth also affirms that God is in all things. He emphasizes that God is free to be inwardly present to all things and that God is "as a gift . . . everywhere, with and *in all* things."[20] For Barth, creation is certainly not without or apart from God. The assertion that God is with creation is indeed central to his doctrine of creation and is expressed in his thesis that the covenant is the internal basis of creation. As he writes, "it would be a strange love that was satisfied with the mere existence and nature of the other, then withdrawing, leaving it to its own devices. Love wills to love."[21] It is central in Barth's thought that the Creator creates a relationship.

Modalism

A third reason that some argue that Barth is inconsistent in his Trinitarian approach to the doctrine of creation is that some believe Barth's concern of safeguarding the unity of God causes him to present God in a modalistic manner in God's relationship with the world. According to Aung, "on the one hand Barth presents God in a trinitarian sense when the subject becomes a question of divine mode of being in His self-revelation and the relationship between the

19. *CD* I/2, 162; II/1, 411, 475–77, 500, and 503. Barth does not go to the extent of Moltmann who speaks of creation as kenosis in the sense of God withdrawing himself to create a space (nothingness) in which God creates the world. See Moltmann, *Trinity and the Kingdom*, 108–11; Moltmann, *God in Creation*, 86–90; and Moltmann, "God's Kenosis," 145–46.

20. *CD* II/1, 485 (emphasis added), cf. 313, 462, 469, and 475–77. At the same time, Barth rejects pantheism and (a certain form of) "panentheism" because God cannot be synthesized with creation (*CD* II/1, 312, 315, and 562).

21. *CD* III/1, 95.

being of God and the creation of the world. On the other hand he presents God in an absolute monotheistic sense when it becomes a question about the unity of God."[22]

Barth is indeed concerned with safeguarding the unity of God. Barth is not, however, a modalist, as more than enough interpreters of Barth have shown.[23] Rather, one's preference for a social doctrine of the Trinity is likely to lead one to critique Barth in this manner. I further consider how Barth presents the Trinity in the context of the work of creation below in this chapter.

Binary Divine Creativity

Finally, some argue that Barth's Trinitarian approach is inconsistent in his discussion of divine activity in creation. That is, Barth's discussion is binary, not Trinitarian, because he only discusses the creative activity of the Father and Son. The Spirit, on the other hand, seems to be missing in the process. Hence, John Webster observes that those who complain that Barth lacks "an adequately triune account of God as creator and God's relation to creation" often do so because they feel something is lacking in Barth's pneumatology.[24] Having considered various critiques of Barth, I turn to examine exactly how Barth expresses the place of the Father, the Son, and the Spirit in the work of creation, particularly with this last critique in mind.

22. Aung, *Doctrine of Creation*, 270. Cf. Moltmann, *Trinity and the Kingdom*, 139.

23. For example, Molnar, *Divine Freedom*, 41 and Hunsinger, "Mysterium Trinitatis," 191.

24. Webster, *Barth*, 111. For example, see Torrance, "Interaction with Karl Barth," 61, and Aung, *Doctrine of Creation*, 269.

THE TRIUNE CREATOR

The Father

Consistent with the creedal tradition, which affirms belief in "God the Father Almighty, maker of heaven and earth," Barth appropriates the work of creation to God the Father.[25] That is, the Father has the dominant role in the work of creation, which makes it most appropriate to identify the Father as the Creator. However, this appropriation does not deny the existence or the roles of the Son and the Spirit in creation. Indeed, creation is not exclusive to the Father because there are not three gods.[26] Barth affirms the Trinitarian maxim *opera trinitatis ad extra sunt indivisa*—the works of the Trinity are indivisible externally.[27] According to Barth, the emphasis on the work of the Father in creation (or on any other divine person in any divine act) is never meant to suggest a separation from the other divine persons. This is clarified especially through the doctrine of *perichoresis*, which "states that the divine modes of being mutually condition and permeate one another so completely that one is always in the other two and the other two in the one." This "implies both a confirmation of the distinction in the modes of being, for none would be what it is (not even the Father) without its co-existence with the others, and also a relativisation of this distinction, for none exists as a special individual, but all three 'in-exist' or exist only in concert as modes of being of the one God and Lord who posits Himself from eternity to eternity."[28] Hence, when Barth (with others in the Christian tradition) speaks

---

25. *CD* I/1, 398; III/1, 11, 49, and *passim*.

26. *CD* III/1, 49.

27. *CD* I/1, 442; III/1, 49.

28. *CD* I/1, 370. Cf. 394 and 442.

of God the Father as the Creator, he means God the Father *with the Son and with the Holy Spirit.* This appropriation speaks of both the intercommunity of the divine persons and their distinctions.

Barth concedes that he does not find the equation of "Father" and "Creator" in Scripture,[29] but he wishes to conform to the creed which first speaks of the act of creation in context of the "Father Almighty." Barth justifies and affirms the appropriation of creation to the Father by means of an analogy of relations, writing that "creation is the temporal analogue, taking place outside God, of that event in God Himself by which God is the Father of the Son."[30] In other words, just as the Father is the eternally unoriginate origin, the Father is also temporally the uncreated Creator. This is an analogy of roles or relations. It is "a reflection, a shadowing forth of this inner divine relationship between God the Father and the Son."[31] Creation is the Father's "originative activity *ad extra.*"[32] Already we begin to see that the role of the Holy Spirit is missing, for Barth only considers the relationship of the Father with the Son in this analogy of relations.[33]

---

29. *CD* III/1, 49. By contrast, in *CD* I/1, 389, he refers to Deuteronomy 32:6 and Isaiah 64:7–8, which both speak of the creative work of the "Father."

30. Barth, *Dogmatics in Outline*, 43. Cf. *CD* III/1, 49.

31. Barth, *Dogmatics in Outline*, 43. Cf. *CD* I/1, 397; and III/1, 49.

32. *CD* III/1, 49.

33. When Barth argues that creation is not necessary because of relationality within God he also focuses only on the relationships of the Father and Son. See *CD* II/1, 667; and III/1, 50, 183.

The Son

In accordance with the doctrine of the Trinity with its accompanying affirmation of the unity of the divine persons, Barth affirms that God the Son participated in the work of creation: "Jesus Christ is the Word by which God created the world out of nothing."[34]

Barth emphasizes that creation is *in*, *for*, and *through* Christ (John 1:3, 10; Col 1:15–17; Heb 1:2).[35] This does not mean that Christ was just an administrator or helper doing the will of the Father. Rather, Barth affirms that Christ was the partner or associate of the Father in creation.[36] Jesus Christ is not an intermediate being between God and creation, but "He is the Mediator between God and man, like the 'wisdom' of the Old Testament."[37] Proclamation of the Son's role in creation is an indirect affirmation of the *homoousios*. Following Athanasius, Barth concludes that if Christ had a part in creation, he must be one essence with the Father.[38] To describe Jesus Christ as Creator is to proclaim him as Lord.

When Barth speaks of the Son as Creator, he means Jesus Christ. He states outright that when "the world came into being, it was created and sustained by the little child that was born in Bethlehem."[39] Barth believes that the New

34. *CD* I/1, 442.

35. *CD* III/1, 51–56.

36. *CD* III/1, 52. This interpretation stands in contrast to Pannenberg's (*Systematic Theology*, vol. 2, 30) as he suggests that according to Barth "the Son's part is simply that it was with a view to the Son that the Father created us humans and our world" and that "Barth says nothing about the Son's own subjectivity" in the act of creation.

37. *CD* III/1, 53.

38. *CD* I/1, 442 and 447.

39. Barth, *Dogmatics in Outline*, 48.

Testament writers and the Christian faith proclaim not simply the eternal Son (or *logos asarkos*—Word apart from flesh) as the Creator, but the incarnate one, Jesus Christ (the *logos ensarkos*—Word *in* flesh)[40] and that this is so because Jesus Christ is the elected one, and this election is the beginning of all of God's works. As the elected one, Jesus Christ "is the eternal archetype and prototype of God's glory in His externalisation, the archetype and prototype of God's co-existence with another."[41] Hence, Barth affirms that Jesus Christ is active in the work of creation.

The Holy Spirit

Clearly Barth should not deny that the Holy Spirit is involved in creation. This conclusion follows from his doctrine of the Trinity. He is explicit in naming the Holy Spirit when speaking of the *identity* of the Creator (but not specifically in connection with God's creative work *ad extra*), writing that

> the God who created heaven and earth is God "the Father," i.e., the Father of Jesus Christ, who as such in eternal generation posits Himself in the Son by the Holy Spirit, and is not therefore in any sense posited from without or elsewhere. It is as this Eternal Father, determined in the act of His free expression and therefore not from without but from within, determining Himself in His Son by the Holy Spirit and Himself positing everything else, that He is also the Creator.[42]

40. *CD* III/1, 56–58. I discuss this point further in the following chapter.

41. *CD* II/1, 667.

42. *CD* III/1, 11.

Barth also affirms that as a divine person, "the Holy Spirit of God is the self-communication of His fatherhood as well as His lordship as Creator, so that without Him God could not partake of the name of Father and Creator."[43] Although this is in the context of creation, it only speaks of the Holy Spirit with respect to the identity of the Creator, but not specifically with respect to the Holy Spirit's work in the act of creating.

Elsewhere, in his discussion of the Trinity (*CD* I/1), Barth comes close to developing a discussion of the Holy Spirit's action in creation. In the New Testament, the life-giving work of the Holy Spirit is portrayed as soterio-eschatological. However, Barth remarks, this New Testament emphasis on the re-creative work of God presupposes the original creative work of the Spirit that is in fact found in the Old Testament. Here the Spirit, the breath of God, is seen as the giver and preserver of life. Hence, Barth affirms that the Holy Spirit is the breath of God by which things were made (Ps 33:6).[44]

It sounds as though Barth is attributing creative work to the Holy Spirit. However when he turns from exposition of Scripture to dogmatics he fails to explicitly state that the Holy Spirit participates in the act of creation. Rather, when discussing the work of creation (*CD* III/1), he speaks of the role of the Holy Spirit in terms of the relation of the Father and the Son. The Holy Spirit is the fundamental condition for the ground of creation, which is "the incarnate Word of God as the content and object of the eternal divine decree of grace."[45] This decree of grace, and the resultant creative will of God, presupposes that "the unity, love and peace between God the Father and Son are not unsettled or

43. *CD* III/1, 49.
44. *CD* I/1, 472.
45. *CD* III/1, 58.

disturbed but transcendently glorified by the fact that the Word of God becomes flesh, that in His Son God takes to Himself man's misery."[46] It is here that Barth finds the role of the Spirit. The Spirit is the unity of the Father and the Son, and glorifies their fellowship. This, and only this, is the work of the Holy Spirit in creation. Only as the communion of the Father and the Son does there exist in the Spirit "the whole order of the relation between God the Creator and His creatures."[47] Barth affirms that "there could be no creature, nor any creation, if God were not also the Holy Spirit and active as such, just as He is also the Father and the Son and active as such."[48] The Holy Spirit is the foundation of the unity between the Father and Son and thus the condition of the creative will and work of the Father and Son.

In Barth's discussion of the work of creation, the role of the Holy Spirit in creation is actually passive. The Holy Spirit is a condition for original creation. Accordingly, as John Thompson interprets Barth's understanding of the Holy Spirit's work in creation, Thompson is only able to speak of the Spirit as the condition, confirmation, and guarantor of creation—"God the Father is the Creator, God the Son, the means and goal of creation, God the Holy Spirit, the one who particularly guarantees its existence."[49] Barth does not directly attribute divine creative activity to the Holy Spirit. While many theologians find a place to do so in their discussion of Genesis 1:2, Barth instead posits that in this text the Spirit brooding over the waters is not something that actually happened, but rather simply a caricature of myth.[50] Barth also does not work out the implications of

46. *CD* III/1, 58.
47. *CD* III/1, 56.
48. *CD* III/1, 58.
49. Thompson, *Holy Spirit*, 160.
50. *CD* III/1, 108.

the Old Testament passages that he refers to regarding the Holy Spirit as giver and preserver of life. Rather, he points to these as confirmation of his view that the Holy Spirit is the foundation for the existence of creation.

Given these observations, one can correctly conclude that there is a binary character to divine creative activity in Barth's doctrine of creation. Nevertheless, Barth does not explicitly deny creative activity of the Holy Spirit, and its affirmation is certainly latent in his doctrine of the Trinity. While there is no hint of modalism in Barth's doctrine of creation, Barth's doctrine of the Trinity does keep Barth from emphasizing the divine creative activity of the Spirit. That is, Barth follows the Augustinian or bestowal model of the Trinity. Hence, with respect to the doctrine of creation, Barth primarily presents the Holy Spirit as the love or unity between the Father and the Son. One account of this, David Guretzki rightly identifies a "systematic overuse of the *filioque* in his [Barth's] doctrine of Creation."[51] By this Guretzki means that in Barth's doctrine of creation, he "tended to theorize from a concept presupposed in the immanent Trinity (i.e., the Spirit as the communion between the Father and the Son by virtue of his eternal procession from both) to the economic Trinity rather than vice versa." In other words, Barth "sought to relate creation and history on the basis of a doctrine of the *filioque* already presupposed."[52] The result is that Barth speaks of Jesus Christ, but not the Holy Spirit, as active in creation with the Father. The Holy Spirit appears only as the foundation of the unity of the Father and Son in the work of creation. Although there is certainly room

51. *Filioque* is a Latin term, meaning "and the Son." The Western church eventually added the word *filioque* to the Nicene-Constantinopolitan Creed in order to say that the Spirit proceeds from the Father "and the Son."

52. Guretzki, *Karl Barth on the* Filioque, 162.

for Barth to develop his pneumatology in his doctrine of creation, one should not condemn Barth too strongly for this lack of development, for he is really only one example among many others in post-Enlightenment Protestantism who have muted the Spirit's activity in creation.[53]

CONCLUSIONS

Some interpreters of Barth's doctrine of creation have suggested that Barth, who is ironically hailed as the father of contemporary Trinitarian theology, is inconsistently Trinitarian in his doctrine of creation. Some have suggested that he should have proposed a threefold understanding of the image of God. However, Barth has correctly interpreted the image of God as relational. And while some interpreters have also suggested that he presents God as separate from the sphere of creation, in particular in a different sphere from the earth (in contrast to heaven), this critique is unsubstantiated, for Barth speaks of God outside creation only to emphasize the Creator/creature distinction. Furthermore, he speaks of creation being in God's space and constantly reminds his readers that God is present with (and for) creation in Jesus Christ and even that God is present in creation. This close relationship between God and creation becomes clear as Barth argues that the covenant is the internal basis of creation: God creates relationship. A third and fourth critique of Barth is that he has modalistic tendencies and presents divine creativity in a binary fashion. Barth is concerned with safeguarding the unity of God, but he is certainly not modalistic. His doctrine of creation is assuredly Trinitarian and he confesses that the identity of the Creator is the triune God. On the other hand, Barth does present

53. Nüssel, "Challenges," 121–22; and Gabriel, *Lord is the Spirit*, 134.

the divine action of creation in a binary fashion. That is, he focuses on the activity of the Father and the Son in creation (though he does not explicitly deny the role of the Holy Spirit in creation). His adherence to the bestowal model of the Trinity leads him to this binary presentation of divine creative action. Accordingly, he speaks of the Father and the Son as creating, but not the Holy Spirit. As the Father is the unoriginate divine person, creation is attributed to God the Father; and since the Son—Jesus Christ—is of the same substance with the Father, creative work is ascribed to the Son; but Barth neglects speaking of the Spirit's activity in creation. Instead he emphasizes the Spirit as the unity between the Father and Son, and therefore as a fundamental condition of creation. Yet for Barth to hold consistently to the doctrine that the works of the Trinity are indivisible externally, he should have also affirmed the creative activity of the Holy Spirit. Jürgen Moltmann was correct to say, "Barth's doctrine of the Trinity is the blueprint of his doctrine of creation, which can be recognized everywhere. Anyone who thinks that this or that part of the structure of his doctrine of creation has to be changed must therefore be in a position to change his doctrine of the Trinity."[54]

To conclude, Barth's doctrine of creation encourages those seeking to form a Trinitarian doctrine of creation 1) to recognize the relational character of "the image of God"; 2) to recognize that although creation was not necessary, God is not removed from his creation but rather is immanent to it and remains in relation to it; and lastly, 3) to recognize that creation, as the work of the one triune God, is a work of unity and love, being affected by the work of each of the divine persons, who are, notably, the same Father, Son, and Holy Spirit who affect salvation. As we have seen, at times Barth emphasizes the eternal relations

54. Moltmann, *History and the Triune God*, 130.

of these divine persons and the implications it has for the doctrine of creation. On account of this, some theologians have suggested that Barth's doctrine of creation does not adequately take account of the created historical reality that God and humanity face. I take up this concern in the next chapter.

5

Jesus, History, and Creation

ONE COMMON CRITIQUE REGARDING Karl Barth's doctrine of creation concerns the place of history, or lack thereof, in this aspect of his work. Critics suggest that he focuses on the eternal and pre-temporal Jesus Christ rather than upon the created historical reality that God and humanity face. Some even suggest that this neglect of history leads Barth to deny creaturely existence. For some, it seems that Barth denies the Creator/creation distinction in his understanding that Christ is the prototype of creation and in his apparent rejection of the *logos asarkos* (Word apart from flesh). In actuality, Barth does still have room in his theology for the concept of the *logos asarkos*. Nevertheless, for Barth, knowledge of creation is found in (the historical) Jesus Christ. Furthermore, when one considers the core of Barth's doctrine of creation, it is difficult to conclude that Barth presents creation in an *a*historical manner because in his creation/covenant thesis he has clearly emphasized a historical relationship that takes place between God and humanity in the covenant.

THE ETERNITY/HISTORY DIALECTIC

G. C. Berkouwer, one of Barth's early interpreters, identified a dialectic between history and eternity in Barth's doctrine of creation, but concluded that Barth displays an unbalanced emphasis on the eternal nature of God's creative work. He identifies this in Barth's emphasis on the priority of the covenant throughout his doctrine of creation. Barth often presents the covenant as pre-history, whereas creation is part of history. The pre-historical nature of the covenant is evident in the prefiguration of reconciliation found in creation (that is, creation is prophetic of, preparation for, and aiming immediately at covenant history). Berkouwer believes this displays the "triumph of grace" in Barth's doctrine of creation.[1] To bring this to light, Berkouwer considers the doctrine of creation before election, reversing Barth's order of placing the doctrine of election before creation in his *Church Dogmatics*. Berkouwer does this because he feels that following this traditional order will show how significant grace—the pre-historical covenant—is in Barth's theology.

Berkouwer's critique of Barth is somewhat indirect in that it appears as a dialogue with Regin Prenter. Prenter, a former pupil of Barth, critiques Barth for the unity he gives to reconciliation and creation. He finds that the result of this is that the significance and decisiveness of history are imperiled. This is because everything with regards to salvation has been completed before creation; it only has to

1. Similarly, Brown (*Karl Barth*, 151) has written of Barth that "all God's dealings with men are effected in and through Jesus Christ through whom grace triumphs over all."

be actualized in history. This makes it difficult to speak of a historical fall, or historical reconciliation. Thus, Prenter accuses Barth of "creation docetism."[2]

Berkouwer believes that Prenter's accusation of "creation docetism" is an unjust criticism of Barth. He notes that Barth affirms the goodness of creation because it is "created *in* Jesus of Nazareth, and exists only in terms of His *saving grace*."[3] Nevertheless, regarding Prenter's primary criticism of Barth, Berkouwer agrees that Barth "points continually to the *unity* of God's work from the viewpoint of its a priori omnipotence and irresistibility, and to the eternity-aspect of that work, through which it becomes impossible to separate creation and redemption in terms of historical stages."[4] However, Berkouwer argues that Prenter is wrong to think that simply separating or disuniting the works of creation and reconciliation will correct the loss of the significance of history in Barth, because God's eternal counsel keeps one from separating the works of creation and reconciliation. Berkouwer writes,

> the real issue raised by Barth's Christological doctrine of creation is not whether his conception may be opposed in terms of the center of the redemptive process, namely, *Jesus* Christ, and therefore by an *historicizing* of the works of

2. Prenter "Die Einheit von Schöpfung und Erlösung," 175, cited in Berkouwer, *Triumph of Grace*, 251.

3. Berkouwer, *Triumph of Grace*, 251 (original emphasis). By comparison, outside of the doctrine of creation, Wingren (*Theology in Conflict*, 23–44 and 108–28) argues that Barth neglects the significance of history in the fact that salvation simply concerns recognition (knowledge) of the revelation of all that which has occurred before creation.

4. Berkouwer, *Triumph of Grace*, 250 (original emphasis). Berkouwer also finds this to be exemplified in Barth's preference for supralapsarianism (ibid., 255–56).

God, but rather whether the unity of God's work
*may ever be presented in antithesis to what Barth
has called the "step-wise" character of God's works
and against which he directs his sharp protest.*[5]

Berkouwer argues that this is precisely what one finds in the
Bible. One finds the Bible presenting God's decisions "from
eternity" along with presenting the unity and omnipotence
of God's works, without devaluing the historical "step-wise"
character of creation and redemption, as seen, for example,
in the transition from death to life as confessed by the
Apostle Paul. Berkouwer cautions that the historical "reaction" to sin must not overshadow the initiative of God's
works prior to sin and that, likewise, God's initiative must
not overshadow his reaction to the fall in history. He writes,
"when it is attempted to construct a *synthesis* of these two
elements which will be perspicuous to our understanding,
it is inevitable that we shall fail to do justice to one or to the
other and that we shall fall into the abyss of either eternal-
izing God's works or historicizing them."[6]

Berkouwer posits that Barth does speak of God's "reaction" to sin, but that God's initiative and predetermined
plan threatens to overshadow the former aspect of Barth's
thought. On this point, Berkouwer comments that "the initiative of grace wholly absorbs the full *historical* significance
of evil because this initiative was itself the reaction which,
according to God's eternal grace, would be *illustratively* revealed in history and in man's confrontation with the power
of the chaos."[7] Thus, Berkouwer suggests that Barth can't
speak of the historical reality of sin without being confront-
ed with "insoluble difficulties and antinomies." Berkouwer

5. Ibid., 252 (original emphasis).

6. Ibid., 253 (original emphasis).

7. Ibid., (original emphasis), cf. 248.

concludes that "within *this* framework of thinking the *decisiveness* of history can no longer be fully honored."[8]

Overall, Berkouwer argues that Barth places an overemphasis on the unity, and thus completion, of God's works before creation to the detriment of history. That is, in contrast to Prenter, Berkouwer does not suggest any major changes to Barth's theology but only suggests a shift in emphasis upon the historical aspect of God's works rather than upon the eternal aspect. Berkouwer does not propose correction but only a critique regarding the significance of history in Barth's doctrine of creation. Berkouwer seems content to affirm the antinomies he feels are found in the Bible, only while emphasizing the historical aspect of reconciliation more than Barth. This seems to be a very limited advance, if it is one at all.

Barth himself has responded to Berkouwer and his response is sufficient for all those who critique Barth's doctrine of creation by saying that he neglects history and the salvation found therein. Against Berkouwer's overall claim that Barth presents the gospel as "the triumph of grace," Barth writes, "we are concerned with the living person of Jesus Christ. Strictly, it is not grace, but He Himself as its Bearer, Bringer and Revealer, who is the Victory, the light which is not overwhelmed by darkness, but before which darkness must yield as it is itself overwhelmed."[9] This response to Berkouwer includes his discussion of Barth's doctrine of creation and those criticisms that claim that all of the salvific work of Christ is completed before creation in Barth's theology. Berkouwer's aim of portraying the triumph of grace in creation as found in Barth causes Berkouwer to place an overemphasis on Barth's doctrine of Nothingness.

8. Ibid., 254–55 (original emphasis). Likewise, Deegan, "Christological Determinant," 120 and 130–35.

9. *CD* IV/3, 173.

In fact, it takes up the majority of his discussion of Barth's doctrine of creation. In contrast, Barth focuses on the covenant of grace in Jesus Christ, by which we come to know of the triumph of grace.

Contrary to Berkouwer's concern, Barth does not present history as purely illustrative, nor is it an ideal history. As noted above, Barth does not focus on a principle of grace, but rather on the works of Jesus Christ. As Edwin Chr. Van Driel observes, for Barth the works of Jesus Christ are not just *revealed* in time, they are *actualized* in time.[10] It is in the historical life of Christ that evil and sin are actually struggled with and defeated. Only in history are evil and sin recognized. This is the true christological thinking of Barth. Expressing the historical significance of Christ, Barth states that there is not already in the doctrine of election "a principle which has priority over the person and work of Jesus Christ," and Jesus Christ is not "understood only as the mighty executive organ of the divine will of grace."[11] Rather, as Barth emphasizes, "to say 'Jesus' is necessarily to say 'history,' His history, the history in which He is what He is and does what He does."[12] Nevertheless, the two aspects of eternity and history still remain in Barth and need to be explained.

According to Barth, God's "time," or eternal "time," is not timelessness. It is the immediate unity of past, present, and future. It is pure duration, having the character of temporality, namely pre-temporality, supra-temporality, and post-temporality.[13] In contradistinction, time is a one-way sequence that is created by God and is relative to God's

10. Driel, *Incarnation Anyway*, 87.

11. *CD* IV/3, 175.

12. *CD* IV/3, 179.

13. *CD* III/1, 67; III/2, 519; II/1, 608–77; and Barth, *Dogmatics in Outline*, 46–47.

eternity. God, on the other hand, is before time, over time, and after time—again, pre-temporal, supra-temporal, and post-temporal. God's eternity is God's "contemporaneity to all times" and God is "the eternal contemporary."[14] George Hunsinger notes that, "Jesus Christ in Barth's theology *is* the unity of time and eternity. Eternity is not to be understood in abstraction from Jesus of Nazareth. . . . Eternity is *defined* as inseparable from the particular temporality of Jesus, as ontologically filled and shaped by it."[15] God's eternity is transcendent of time, but also includes time. It is "perichoretic not only in itself, but also in its reception of history."[16] According to this understanding of time one sees that God is eternally loving, able, and intending to overcome evil and sin. Further, one understands that evil and sin are not a threat to God. They still exist and are overcome *in history* by Jesus Christ as he fulfills the eternal will of God. This means that there is no antinomy between eternity and history in Barth (contrary to Berkouwer's suggestion). Rather, evil and sin are overcome in history, which God eternally anticipates. With regards to Jesus, his life remains in Barth thoroughly historical.[17] This leads us to our second main point.

14. Gunton, "Salvation," 156, and Langdon, *God the Eternal Contemporary.*

15. Hunsinger, *How to Read Karl Barth*, 16–17. Hunsinger expounds this further in "Mysterium Trinitatis," 186–209.

16. Hunsinger, *How to Read Karl Barth*, 241. Cf. *CD*, II/1, 45 and 396.

17. Cf. Jenson who writes regarding Christ that "In *our* history God makes His *eternal* decision," in *Alpha and Omega*, 163 (original emphasis).

THE CREATOR/CREATION DISTINCTION AND THE *LOGOS ASARKOS*

Although Barth certainly affirms the Creator/creation distinction (at least explicitly),[18] some have argued that Barth's (supposed) neglect of history logically implies a denial of the Creator/creation distinction. Like Berkouwer, Gordon Watson comes to the conclusion that Barth has neglected history in forming his doctrine of creation. Watson summarizes Barth's doctrine of creation in the assertion that the act of revelation in Jesus presupposes all distinctions in God and God with the creature. He continues by asking if Barth's method of understanding God and the creature in the light of Jesus Christ provides an adequate basis for affirming the Creator/creation distinction and to affirm that creation is not necessary. This would establish the created integrity of the world. His premise is that in order to affirm the Creator/creation distinction, one must distinguish between the eternal generation of the Son and his incarnation in time.[19] This is, again, an issue of the significance of history.

On this point a number of theologians have concluded that Barth's analysis of the doctrine of creation is inadequate. Barth proposes that, as the elected one, Jesus Christ "is the eternal archetype and prototype of God's glory in His externalisation, the archetype and prototype of God's co-existence with another."[20] The potential problem with Barth's position is that if the created nature of Jesus Christ is thought to be prototypical for creation, then the human nature of Christ no longer appears to be a created nature

18. See chapter 2. Young, *Creator, Creation and Faith*, 95, even speaks of a so-called "secular integrity" of the world within Barth's doctrine of creation.

19. Watson, *God and the Creature*, 136 and 165–68.

20. *CD* II/1, 667.

(since it exists before creation). Thus, creation (which follows the "prototype" of Christ's created existence) no longer appears to have a nature distinct from God.[21]

The weight of this critique becomes stronger since some of Barth's statements make it seem as though he rejects the doctrine of the *logos asarkos* (Word apart from flesh), which seems to support the conclusion that in Barth's mind the created nature of Jesus existed eternally. Barth once commented,

> No, the incarnation makes no change in the Trinity. In the *eternal decree* of God, Christ is God and man. Do not ever think of the second Person of the Trinity as only *Logos.* . . . There is no *Logos asarkos*, but only *ensarkos.* . . . Since there is only and always a *Logos ensarkos* [Word in flesh], there is no change in the Trinity, as if a fourth member comes in after the incarnation.[22]

Comparable statements in the *Church Dogmatics* indicate the same idea. For example, within his doctrine of creation he writes, "from all *eternity* God turned *to the creature* in the person of His Son."[23] On account of such statements, some have concluded that Barth altogether rejects the concept of the *logos asarkos* and that Barth, therefore, is claiming that the incarnation existed, and flesh existed, in eternity before creation.[24] In other words, for some

21. Mueller, *Karl Barth*, 152; Idinopulos, "Critical Weakness," 162, 165; and Watson, *God and the Creature*, v, 165–68. For some, this is too close to a Christian form of Platonism. See Hendry, "Transcendental Method," 213–27; Aung, *Doctrine of Creation*, 41; and Deegan, "Christological Determinant," 129.

22. Barth, *Table Talk*, 49 (original emphasis).

23. *CD* III/1, 76 (emphasis added).

24. Waldrop, *Karl Barth's Christology*, 46 and Jenson, "Karl Barth," 39.

theologians Barth's affirmations that the *logos ensarkos* is eternal and that the incarnation makes no change in God logically implies Christ's created nature is eternal. To reiterate, the concern here is the need to affirm the Creator/creature distinction. However, the supposed ahistorical nature of the incarnation leads some of Barth's interpreters to claim that Barth has not established the created integrity of the world.

In actuality, Barth affirms the historicity of the incarnation for he does not argue that the incarnation is eternal and he does not altogether reject the concept of the *logos asarkos*. In his doctrine of creation Barth states that it was Jesus Christ who was the Creator, not the *logos asaskos*, if by *logos asarkos* one means "a formless Christ who might well be a Christ-principle or something of that kind."[25] Barth's concern is that the concept of the *logos asarkos* is abstract. In contrast, he wants to affirm that *Jesus* (not some abstract idea of the *logos*) is the Creator—Jesus, through whom the kingdom of God comes near and Jesus as the one who is the fulfillment of the covenant. Barth insists that when biblical texts speak of creation occurring in and through Christ (John 1:3; Heb 1:2; and Col 1:15) they are not speaking of a *logos asarkos*. Rather, they are concerned with the Word-made-flesh and, more specifically, they are aimed at affirming that Jesus Christ is the Lord who creates all things in conformity with his eternal will and purpose. In asserting that one should speak of Jesus, rather than the *logos asarkos*, as Creator, Barth is not completely rejecting the doctrine of the *logos asarkos*. He explicitly affirms that the concept of the *logos asarkos* is "necessary to the christological and trinitarian reflections of the Church" and that "it is indispensable for dogmatic enquiry and presentation."[26] This af-

25. *CD* III/1, 54.
26. *CD* III/1, 54.

firmation of the *logos asarkos* is not, as Paul Jones supposes, only "a qualifying aside" in Barth's doctrine of creation, for Barth even acknowledges that the concept of the *logos asarkos* "is often touched upon in the New Testament."[27]

Barth's interpretation of the *logos asarkos* and its relation to Jesus as Creator remains consistent as Barth continues to develop his theology. Again in *CD* IV/1 (a volume on the doctrine of reconciliation), Barth writes, on the one hand, that when speaking of creation one "must not refer to the second 'person' of the Trinity as such, to the eternal Son or the eternal Word of God *in abstracto*, and therefore to the so-called *logos asarkos*."[28] On the other hand, Barth again clarifies that the concept of the *logos asarkos* is "a necessary and important concept in Trinitarian doctrine when we have to understand the revelation and dealings of God in the light of their *free basis* in the inner being and essence of God."[29] To summarize, Barth affirms the *logos asarkos* as a means of affirming divine freedom, but he wants to emphasize that as God turns to creation there is no *logos asarkos* if that means a concept of a *logos* not shaped by the revelation of God in Jesus Christ—a revelation that clarifies that God is eternally for us.

In his deliberations regarding creation and the *logos asarkos* Barth does not intend to suggest that the incarnation existed before creation. Indeed, Barth affirms that the incarnation only came about in history.[30] Rather, Barth's

---

27. Jones, *Humanity of Christ*, 92 fn. 69; then *CD* III/1, 54. In contrast to Jones, those who recognize that Barth does maintain that there is a legitimate place for the concept of the *logos asarkos* include Molnar, *Divine Freedom*, 71; McCormack, "Grace and Being," 96; and Driel, *Incarnation Anyway*, 95.

28. *CD* IV/1, 52.

29. *CD* IV/1, 52 (emphasis added).

30. *CD* II/1, 515; and III/1, 26, 50, 56.

concern is, first of all, epistemological. He is concerned that the concept of the *logos asarkos* is an "empty concept," which one might "feel obliged to fill with all kinds of contents of our own arbitrary invention" and, thereby, create a speculative image of God apart from the revelation of God in Christ.[31] In this sense, Barth is continuing his rejection of natural theology. Barth's concern is not just epistemological, however. He is also concerned with divine ontology. That is, Barth affirms that the identity of the divine being (and the identity of the *logos* specifically) is shaped by God's eternal self-determination in divine election to be God-for-us. Barth expresses this idea in his doctrine of divine election where he maintains that *Jesus Christ* is not only the object of election, but also the subject of election.[32] Since Jesus is eternally the one who is for us, Barth can affirm that the *logos* becomes incarnate in history without any ontological change and without any division "between His being and essence in Himself and His activity and work as Reconciler of the world created by Him."[33] Hence, as Bruce McCormack observes, for Barth, the *logos* is always the *logos incarnandus* (the *logos* "to be incarnate"), even prior to enfleshment in history.[34] Since the incarnation is eternally anticipated but not yet actualized, it is also true that Christ's human nature (as a part of creation) is also anticipated but not yet actualized.[35] Hence, Barth's discussion of the *logos asarkos* does not jeopardize the Creator/creation distinction.

31. *CD* IV/1, 52, cf. 181.

32. *CD* II/2, 94–145.

33. *CD* IV/1, 184.

34. McCormack, "Grace and Being," 94 and 97. Cf. Thompson, *Christ in Perspective*, 23 and 99; Brown, "Barth's Doctrine of the Creation," 100; and Scott, "Covenant," 184.

35. On the distinction between anticipation, recapitulation, and synchronicity in relation to Barth's view of God's eternity, see

Having demonstrated that Barth does not altogether reject a concept of the *logos asarkos*, and that Barth therefore does not jeopardize the Creator/creation distinction as he expresses his concerns regarding the *logos asarkos*, I turn to consider how understanding the meaning of the covenant in Barth's doctrine of creation should remove any concern that Barth's view of creation is ahistorical.

CONCERNING THE COVENANT

If one is to rightly grasp the historical nature of Barth's doctrine of creation one must grasp the meaning of the covenant given that this concept is central for Barth's doctrine of creation. Many of the critiques of Barth's doctrine of creation in this area have resulted from a misunderstanding of what Barth means by covenant. It is not an ideal concept that exists with only the possibility of being actualized. Covenant is history, that is, a sequence of events.

For Barth the covenant refers to a relationship between God and humanity (and to some extent a relationship between God and all of creation—see chapter 3). It is expressed in God's pronouncement, "I will be your God, and you will be my people." This relationality is a central idea of covenant, which is at the center of Barth's doctrine of creation. John Webster notes that the intention of covenant is "for free responsive life with God, for partnership with the divine Counterpart."[36] Accordingly, when Barth discusses the relationship of Adam and Eve to the tree of the knowledge of good and evil he notes that God does not stop them from partaking of the tree's fruit because God wills fellowship. That is, God wishes for humans to confirm

---

Langdon, *God the Eternal Contemporary*, 34–35 and 110–13.

36. Webster, *Barth*, 111.

God's election.[37] The covenant originates before creation in God's desire "to hold communion with man."[38] It is "partnership in which He has predestined and called man."[39]

This covenant relationship is fulfilled in Jesus Christ. Barth writes that "by covenant we mean Jesus Christ" and that the covenant "became inconceivably true and real in Jesus Christ."[40] As noted above, this is not just an ideal Christ that exists before creation. It is the incarnation and atoning work of Jesus Christ that "is the affirmation and consummation of the institution of the covenant between Himself and man."[41] Accordingly Barth relates Jesus Christ with the covenant in as much as he affirms that Jesus Christ is the beginning and the goal of creation. Since Jesus Christ fulfills the covenant, Barth can even say that "Jesus Christ and His Church are the internal basis of creation."[42] The covenant is God with us and for us.

The covenant relationship as fulfilled in Jesus Christ takes place in the salvation history in which God is for us. The covenant is the "covenant of grace."[43] Barth writes that the covenant is the content of the divine work of reconciliation. In contrast to John Thompson's reading of Barth, Barth does not wish to say that reconciliation is the purpose of creation because Barth feels this implies that creation is the cause of reconciliation.[44] Rather, the covenant is the

---

37. *CD* III/1, 272.

38. Barth, *Dogmatics in Outline*, 54. Cf. *CD* I/1, 273–74.

39. *CD* III/1, 43.

40. Barth, *Dogmatics in Outline*, 54. Cf. *CD* II/2, 8.

41. *CD* IV/1, 36.

42. *CD* III/1, 322; cf. 42, 90, 111, 232, 376; and II/1, 667.

43. *CD* III/1, 43.

44. Thompson, *Christ in Perspective*, 118. *CD* III/1, 47.

presupposition of reconciliation.[45] Nevertheless, in "salvation" terms Barth writes,

> The ordaining of salvation for man and of man for salvation is the original and basic will of God, the ground and purpose of His will as Creator. It is not that He first wills and works the being of the world and man, and then ordains it to salvation. But God creates, preserves and over-rules man for this prior end and with this prior purpose, that there may be a being distinct from Himself ordained for salvation, for perfect being, for participation in His own being, because as the One who loves in freedom He has determined to exercise redemptive grace—and that there may be an object of this His redemptive grace, a partner to receive it.[46]

Barth is not quite as explicit regarding the relation of covenant and salvation in *Church Dogmatics* III/1 but the relation is still expressed.[47]

For Barth covenant is clearly a historical happening. The covenant commences "immediately after creation."[48] It might seem that Barth is a little unclear regarding when exactly this is since he speaks of covenant history "commencing with the fall"[49] while at the same time speaking of God's rest (on the seventh day of creation) as marking the beginning of the history of the covenant;[50] however, Barth regards these stories as sagas, not as literal history.

---

45. *CD* IV/1, 22–66.

46. *CD* IV/1, 9–10; and IV/2, 760.

47. *CD* III/1, 46, 59. There still remains however a distinction between salvation and covenant. See *CD* III/1, 71.

48. *CD* III/1, 75 and 190.

49. *CD* III/1, 241; cf. 109 and 289.

50. *CD* III/1, 98, 217, and 218. He also says that the covenant

Regardless, it is clear that he views creation as the way to the covenant. This is expressed in the "external" portion of his thesis—creation is the external basis of the covenant, that is, there has to be a creation for God to relate to for there to be a covenant. Historically speaking, then, the covenant occurs after creation. At the same time, Barth also speaks of God covenanting with humanity during the history of creation. For example, he writes, "the second creation saga embraces both the history of creation and that of the covenant."[51] Barth even speaks of the blessing of animals as an aspect of covenant history.[52] Accordingly, creation is not only the enabling of the covenant. It is part of the covenant itself. The covenant takes place, then, both in creation history and after creation history.

At the same time, without being inconsistent, Barth speaks of the covenant as existing before creation. He writes, "the covenant is not only quite as old as creation; it is older than it."[53] It existed before the world. Here one again finds a close connection between covenant and election in Barth's thinking. Covenant is the actualization of God's eternal election in history. Covenant is not simply the equivalent of election, however. Otherwise Barth would not have bothered to differentiate between the two. Election is in pre-temporal eternity.[54] This election happens before creation and the love that is expressed in it overflows into creation. Covenant is more than this election. Nev-

---

"commences with Abraham" but then, in a seemingly intentional manner he immediately corrects himself and says "or rather is revealed in Abraham as the history of God with man, as the execution of God's covenant with the earth" (*CD* III/1, 151).

51. *CD* III/1, 240. Cf. I/1, 142; III/1, 42, 47, 237; and IV/1, 36.

52. *CD* III/1, 170.

53. Barth, *Dogmatics in Outline*, 46; and *CD* III/4, 39–40.

54. *CD* II/2, 104.

ertheless, ontologically speaking, the covenant does exist before creation. The internal basis of creation is, therefore, *"the eternal covenant* which God has decreed in Himself as the covenant of the Father with His Son."[55] To summarize, according to Barth, the covenant takes place historically both in and after creation history, but the covenant also exists ontologically before creation. In other words, temporally covenant history begins with creation history; however, the covenant is anticipated before this history.

To summarize Barth's view of the covenant, the covenant refers to a relationship between God and humanity as fulfilled in Jesus Christ in salvation history. Having recognized this, one must again remember that at the center of Barth's doctrine of creation is the affirmation that the covenant is the ground and goal of creation. This is expressed in Barth's theses that creation is the external basis of the covenant and covenant is the internal basis of creation. This essentially means that God creates because of the covenant. When one considers this core of Barth's doctrine of creation one cannot be led to the conclusion that Barth views creation as ahistorical, because Barth has clearly emphasized a historical relationship that takes place between God and humanity in the covenant. Covenant is not a question of a static relationship in eternity but a historical relationship in which God freely loves his creation.

CONCLUSION

Some theologians critique Barth for neglecting the significance of history in his doctrine of creation. One finds a common claim that he focuses on the eternal and pre-temporal Jesus Christ (who is the fulfillment of the

---

55. *CD* III/1, 97 (emphasis added).

covenant) rather than upon the created reality God and humanity face. Barth's assertion that the *logos ensarkos* pre-existed creation might seem to support this claim. In order to affirm the Creator/creation distinction, one must clearly affirm the doctrine of the *logos asarkos* along with the doctrine of the *logos ensarkos*. As we have seen, Barth does affirm both of these doctrines and he bases his knowledge of creation on (the historical) Jesus Christ. Furthermore, for Barth, the internal basis of creation is the covenant, which he understands in a thoroughly historical manner. Hence, Barth takes full account of history in his thesis that creation is the external basis of the covenant and the covenant is the internal basis of creation.

6

Conclusion

BARTH HAS SUCCESSFULLY PRESENTED a doctrine of creation from within the Christian church, taking account of the Trinitarian doctrine salvation as revealed in Jesus Christ. Following historic Christian tradition, Barth affirms the love and freedom of the Creator as he draws together the doctrines of creation and salvation. With respect to the latter, for Barth, creation is the external basis of the covenant and the covenant is the internal basis of creation. On account of the connection between creation and the covenant, Barth affirms not only that creation is distinct from God, but also, in the midst of a world ravaged by war, he confidently declares that creation, as grounded in the divine Yes and as directed to the covenant, is good. While Barth's presentation of the doctrine of creation is dogmatically theological, this should not inhibit one from bringing his insights into dialogue with other scholarly disciplines, including the natural sciences.

Barth's doctrine of creation is unique primarily for the christological emphasis one finds throughout his explication of this doctrine. For example, he claims that the secret of creation is only revealed in Jesus Christ, which leads him to his rejection of natural theology. He also takes a uniquely christological approach to the historic doctrine of *creatio ex nihilo* as he develops the doctrine by drawing an analogy between God's summons in the resurrection and God's summons in the work of creation. Furthermore, Barth insists that *Jesus* is the Creator, not an abstract *logos*, in order to establish that the Jesus, the man from Galilee, is indeed Lord of creation.

While Barth has done well in presenting a christological emphasis in his doctrine of creation, chapters 3 and 4 have demonstrated that those who follow Barth should aim to add more pneumatological reflections to their doctrines of creation by emphasizing both the work of the Holy Spirit in creation as well as the relationship between the Holy Spirit and nature. These pneumatological reflections on creation will not only make one's doctrine of creation more thoroughly Trinitarian than Barth's explication of the doctrine, but they will also assist in developing a theology of nature or ecological theology.

Even though, Barth's doctrine of creation is anthropocentric, those working on a theology of nature or ecological theology would be wise to take account of Barth's doctrine of creation. First of all, one should take caution of the factors that have led Barth to develop his doctrine with a focus on humanity. Second, one can find insights in Barth's doctrine to build upon. In particular, Barth asserts that the whole of creation is that which God wanted, and therefore good; that all of creation participates in the covenant; that creation that is ordered toward right relationships, including human relationships with nature; and that God creates humanity as gardeners who are responsible to serve the earth.

Many have lauded Barth's doctrine of creation for returning to a Trinitarian approach to this doctrine. In this respect, Barth has done better christologically than pneumatologically. One may justifiably critique Barth for not adequately developing his pneumatology in the context of his doctrine of creation (and for his overly systematic application of the *filioque* that did not encourage this development). Nevertheless, Barth does offer many insights that can aid those developing a Trinitarian doctrine of creation. Barth's own presentation of this doctrine encourages those seeking to form a Trinitarian doctrine of creation to take account of the relational character of "the image of God" and to recognize that although creation was not necessary, God is not removed from his creation, but rather is immanent to it and remains in relation to it. In addition, his doctrine of creation encourages those who follow him to expound on the work of the one triune God in creation as a work of unity and love, being affected by the work of each of the divine persons, who are, notably, the same Father, Son, and Holy Spirit who affect salvation. In addition, following Barth's interpretation of Scripture, one can affirm that *Jesus* is the Creator while also making room for a doctrine of the *logos asarkos* in order to consistently affirm the Creator/creation distinction as well as the freedom of God.

Overall, Barth has done well in presenting a Christian doctrine of creation by expanding on what it means that creation was by, for, and in Christ. In Barth's words, "the covenant between God and man is the meaning and the glory, the ground and goal of heaven and earth and the whole creation."[1]

---

1. Barth, *Dogmatics in Outline*, 50.

Bibliography

Aung, Salai Hla. *The Doctrine of Creation in the Theology of Barth, Moltmann and Pannenberg: Creation in Theological, Ecological and Philosophical-Scientific Perspective*. Regensburg: Roderer, 1998.

Balthasar, Hans Urs von. *The Theology of Karl Barth*. Translated by John Drury. New York: Holt, Rinehart and Winston, 1971.

Barbour, Ian G. *When Science Meets Religion: Enemies, Strangers, or Partners?* San Francisco: HarperSanFrancisco, 2000.

Barth, Karl. *Church Dogmatics*. Translation Edited by G. W. Bromiley and T. F. Torrance. 4 vols. Edinburgh: T. & T. Clark, 1956–75.

———. *Dogmatics in Outline*. Translated by G. T. Thomson. London: SCM, 1949.

———. *The Holy Spirit and the Christian Life*. Translated by R. Birch Hoyle. Louisville: Westminster John Knox, 1993.

———. *The Humanity of God*. Translated by John Newton Thomas and Thomas Wieser. Richmond, VA: John Knox, 1960.

———. *Karl Barth's Table Talk*. Recorded and edited by John D. Godsey. Scottish Journal of Theology Occasional Papers 10. Edinburgh: Oliver and Boyd, 1963.

Berkhof, Hendrikus. *Christian Faith: An Introduction to the Study of the Faith*. Translated by Sierd Woudstra. Grand Rapids: Eerdmans, 1979.

Berkouwer, G. C. *The Triumph of Grace in the Theology of Karl Barth*. Translated by Harry R. Boer. London: Paternoster, 1956.

Bromiley, G. W. "Karl Barth." In *Creative Minds in Contemporary Theology*, edited by Philip Edgcumbe Hughes, 27–59. Grand Rapids: Eerdmans, 1966.

Bibliography

Brown, Colin. *Karl Barth and the Christian Message*. London: Tyndale, 1967.

———. "Karl Barth's Doctrine of the Creation." *The Churchman* 76 (1962) 99–105.

Busch, Eberhard. *The Great Passion: An Introduction to Karl Barth's Theology*. Translated by Geoffrey W. Bromiley. Grand Rapids: Eerdmans, 2004.

———. *Karl Barth: His Life from Letters and Autobiographical Texts*. Translated by John Bowden. Philadelphia: Fortress, 1976.

Chung, Paul S. "Karl Barth and God in Creation: Towards an Interfaith Dialogue with Science and Religion." *Theology and Science* 3.1 (2005) 55–70.

Cootsona, Gregory S. *God and the World: A Study in the Thought of Alfred North Whitehead and Karl Barth*. International Theology 6. Frankfurt am Main: Lang, 2001.

Crisp, Oliver D. "Karl Barth on Creation." In *Retrieving Doctrine: Explorations in Reformed Theology*, 26–44. Milton Keynes, UK: Paternoster, 2010.

Deegan, Dan L. "The Christological Determinant in Barth's Doctrine of Creation." *Scottish Journal of Theology* 14 (1961) 119–35.

Driel, Edwin Chr. van. *Incarnation Anyway: Arguments for Supralapsarian Christology*. AAR Academy Series. Oxford: Oxford University Press, 2008.

Frykberg, Elizabeth. *Karl Barth's Theological Anthropology: An Analogical Critique Regarding Gender Relations*. Studies in Reformed Theology and History, vol. 1.3. Princeton: Princeton Theological Seminary, 1993.

Fulljames, Peter. *God and Creation in Intercultural Perspective: Dialogue between the Theologies of Barth, Dickson, Pobee, Nyamiti and Pannenberg*. Studies in the Intercultural History of Christianity 86. Frankfurt am Main: Lang, 1993.

Gabriel, Andrew K. *The Lord is the Spirit: The Holy Spirit and the Divine Attributes*. Eugene, OR: Pickwick, 2011.

———. "Pneumatological Perspectives for a Theology of Nature: The Holy Spirit in Relation to Ecology and Technology." *Journal of Pentecostal Theology* 15.2 (2007) 195–212.

———. "A Trinitarian Doctrine of Creation?: Considering Barth as a Guide." *McMaster Journal of Theology and Ministry* 6 (2005) 36–48.

Godsey, John D. "The Architecture of Karl Barth's *Church Dogmatics*." In *Karl Barth's Table Talk*, edited by John D. Godsey, 1–18. Scottish Journal of Theology Occasional Papers 10. Edinburgh: Oliver and Boyd, 1963.

Gunton, Colin E. "Salvation." In *The Cambridge Companion to Karl Barth*, edited by John Webster, 143–58. Cambridge: Cambridge University Press, 2000.

———. "The Spirit Moved Over the Face of the Waters: The Holy Spirit and the Created Order." *International Journal of Systematic Theology* 4 (2002) 190–204.

———. *The Triune Creator: A Historical and Systematic Study.* Grand Rapids: Eerdmans, 1998.

Guretzki, David. *Karl Barth on the Filioque.* Barth Studies. Burlington, VT: Ashgate, 2009.

Hartwell, Herbert. *The Theology of Karl Barth: An Introduction.* London: Duckworth, 1964.

Hefner, Philip J. "The Creation." In *Christian Dogmatics*, edited by Carl E. Braaten and Robert W. Jenson, 265–358. Minneapolis: Fortress, 1984.

Hendry, George. "The Transcendental Method in the Theology of Karl Barth." *Scottish Journal of Theology* 37 (1984) 213–27.

Henry, Martin. "Karl Barth on Creation." *Irish Theological Quarterly* 69 (2004) 219–23.

Hielema, Syd. "Searching for Disconnected Wires: Karl Barth's Doctrine of Creation Revisited." *Calvin Theological Journal* 30 (1995) 75–93.

Hunsinger, George. *How to Read Karl Barth: The Shape of His Theology.* New York: Oxford University Press, 1991.

———. "Mysterium Trinitatis: Karl Barth's Conception of Eternity." In *Disruptive Grace: Studies in the Theology of Karl Barth*, 186–209. Grand Rapids: Eerdmans, 2000.

Idinopulos, Thomas A. "The Critical Weakness of Creation in Barth's Theology." *Encounter* 33 (1972) 159–69.

Jenson, Robert W. *Alpha and Omega: A Study in the Theology of Karl Barth.* New York: Thomas Nelson, 1963.

———. "Creator and Creature." *International Journal of Systematic Theology* 4.2 (2002) 216–21.

———. "Karl Barth." In *The Modern Theologians: An Introduction to Christian Theology in the Twentieth Century*, Vol. 1, edited by David Ford, 23–49. Oxford: Blackwell, 1989.

Johnson, Elizabeth A. *Women, Earth, and Creator Spirit.* New York: Paulist, 1993.

Johnson, Keith L. *Karl Barth and the Analogia Entis.* T. & T. Clark Studies in Systematic Theology. London: T. & T. Clark, 2010.

Jones, Paul D. *The Humanity of Christ: Christology in Karl Barth's Church Dogmatics.* London: T. & T. Clark, 2008.

Bibliography

Krötke, Wolf. *Sin and Nothingness in the Theology of Karl Barth.* Translated and edited by Philip G. Ziegler and Christina-Maria Bammel. Studies in Reformed Theology and History, New Series 10. Princeton: Princeton Theological Seminary, 2005.

Langdon, Adrian. *God the Eternal Contemporary: Trinity, Eternity, and Time in Karl Barth.* Eugene, OR: Wipf and Stock, 2012.

Lønning, Per. *Creation—An Ecumenical Challenge?: Reflections Issuing from a Study by the Institute for Ecumenical Research Strasbourg, France.* Macon, GA: Mercer University Press, 1989.

Lossky, Vladimir. *Orthodox Theology: An Introduction.* Translated by Ian and Ihita Kesarcodi-Watson. Crestwood, NY: St. Vladimir's Seminary Press, 1978.

MacDonald, Nathan. "The *Imago Dei* and Election: Reading Genesis 1:26–28 and Old Testament Scholarship with Karl Barth." *International Journal of Systematic Theology* 10.3 (2008) 303–27.

Mangina, Joseph L. *Karl Barth: Theologian of Christian Witness.* Louisville: Westminster John Knox, 2004.

McCormack, Bruce L. "Grace and Being: The Role of God's Gracious Election in Karl Barth's Theological Ontology." In *The Cambridge Companion to Karl Barth*, edited by John Webster, 92–110. Cambridge: Cambridge University Press, 2000.

———. *Karl Barth's Critically Realistic Dialectical Theology: Its Genesis and Development 1909–1936.* Oxford: Clarendon, 1995.

———. "Karl Barth's Version of an 'Analogy of Being': A Dialectical No and Yes to Roman Catholicism." In *The Analogy of Being: Invention of the Antichrist or the Wisdom of God?*, edited by Thomas Joseph White, 88–144. Grand Rapids: Eerdmans, 2011.

McKim, Donald K., editor. *How Karl Barth Changed My Mind.* Grand Rapids: Eerdmans, 1986.

McLean, Stuart. "Creation and Anthropology." In *Theology Beyond Christendom: Essays on the Centenary of the Birth of Karl Barth May 10, 1886*, edited by John Thompson, 111–42. Allison Park, PA: Pickwick, 1986.

Metzger, Paul Louis. *The Word of Christ and the World of Culture: Sacred and Secular through the Theology of Karl Barth.* Grand Rapids: Eerdmans, 2003.

Meynell, Hugo A. *Grace versus Nature: Studies in Karl Barth's Church Dogmatics.* London: Sheed and Ward, 1965.

Molnar, Paul D. *Divine Freedom and the Doctrine of the Immanent Trinity: In Dialogue with Karl Barth and Contemporary Theology.* London: T. & T. Clark, 2002.

Moltmann, Jürgen. *God in Creation: An Ecological Doctrine of Creation*. Translated by Margaret Kohl. London: SCM, 1985.

———. "God's Kenosis in the Creation and Consummation of the World." In *The Work of Love: Creation as Kenosis*, edited by John Polkinghorne, 137–51. Grand Rapids: Eerdmans, 2001.

———. *History and the Triune God: Contributions to Trinitarian Theology*. Translated by John Bowden. London: SCM, 1991.

———. *The Trinity and the Kingdom of God: The Doctrine of God*. Translated by Margaret Kohl. London: SCM, 1981.

Mueller, David L. *Karl Barth*. Makers of the Modern Theological Mind. Waco, TX: Word, 1972.

Nimmo, Paul T. "The Orders of Creation in the Theological Ethics of Karl Barth." *Scottish Journal of Theology* 60.1 (2007) 24–35.

Nüssel, Friederike. "Challenges of a Consistent Christian Language for the Creativity of God's Spirit." In *The Spirit in Creation and New Creation: Science and Theology in Western and Orthodox Realms*, edited by Michael Welker, 120–33. Grand Rapids: Eerdmans, 2012.

Pannenberg, Wolfhart. *Systematic Theology*. Vol. 2. Translated by Geoffrey W. Bromiley. Grand Rapids: Eerdmans, 1994.

Peters, Ted. *God as Trinity: Relationality and Temporality in Divine Life*. Louisville: Westminster John Knox, 1993.

Prenter, Regin. "Die Einheit von Schöpfung und Erlösung: Zur Schöpfungslehre Karl Barths." *Theologische Zeitschrift* 2.3 (1946) 161–82.

Price, Daniel J. *Karl Barth's Anthropology in Light of Modern Thought*. Grand Rapids: Eerdmans, 2002.

Richardson, Kurt Anders. *Reading Karl Barth: New Directions for North American Theology*. Grand Rapids: Baker Academic, 2004.

Russell, Robert John. *Cosmology—From Alpha to Omega: The Creative Mutual Interaction of Theology and Science*. Theology and the Sciences. Minneapolis: Fortress, 2008.

Santmire, H. Paul. *Brother Earth: Nature, God, and Ecology in Time of Crisis*. New York: Nelson, 1970.

———. "Creation and Nature: A Study of the Doctrine of Nature with Special Attention to Barth's Doctrine of Creation." ThD diss., Harvard University, 1966.

———. *Nature Reborn: The Ecological and Cosmic Promise of Christian Theology*. Theology and the Sciences. Minneapolis: Fortress, 2000.

———. *Ritualizing Nature: Renewing Christian Liturgy in a Time of Crisis*. Theology and the Sciences. Minneapolis: Fortress, 2008.

Bibliography

————. *The Travail of Nature: The Ambiguous Ecological Promise of Christian Theology*. Philadelphia: Fortress, 1985.

Schwarz, Hans. *Creation*. Grand Rapids: Eerdmans, 2002.

Scott, J. L. "The Covenant in the Theology of Karl Barth." *Scottish Journal of Theology* 17 (1964) 189–98.

Sherman, Robert J. *The Shift to Modernity: Christ and the Doctrine of Creation in the Theologies of Schleiermacher and Barth*. London: T. & T. Clark, 2005.

Tanner, Kathryn. "Creation and Providence." In *The Cambridge Companion to Karl Barth*, edited by John Webster, 111–26. Cambridge: Cambridge University Press, 2000.

Thompson, John. *Christ in Perspective: Christological Perspectives in the Theology of Karl Barth*. Grand Rapids: Eerdmans, 1978.

————. *The Holy Spirit in the Theology of Karl Barth*. Princeton Theological Monograph Series 23. Allison Park, PA: Pickwick, 1991.

Torrance, Iain. "The Trinity in Relation to Creation and Incarnation." *Neue Zeitschrift für Systematische Theologie und Religionsphilosophie* 38 (1996) 29–37.

Torrance, Thomas F. *Karl Barth: Biblical and Evangelical Theologian*. Edinburgh: T. & T. Clark, 1990.

————. "My Interaction with Karl Barth." In *How Karl Barth Changed My Mind*, edited by Donald K. McKim, 52–64. Grand Rapids: Eerdmans, 1986.

————. *Space, Time and Incarnation*. London: Oxford University Press, 1969.

Waldrop, Charles T. *Karl Barth's Christology: Its Basic Alexandrian Character*. New York: Mouton, 1984.

Watson, Gordon. *God and the Creature: The Trinity and Creation in Karl Barth*. Brisbane: Uniting Church Print, 1995.

Webster, John. *Barth*. Outstanding Christian Thinkers. London: Continuum, 2000.

————. *Barth's Ethics of Reconciliation*. Cambridge: Cambridge University Press, 1995.

Whitehouse, Walter Alexander. *Creation, Science, and Theology: Essays in Response to Karl Barth*. Edited by Ann Loades. Grand Rapids: Eerdmans, 1981.

————. "Karl Barth on 'The Work of Creation': A Reading of *Church Dogmatics, III/1*." In *Reckoning with Barth: Essays in Commemoration of the Centenary of Karl Barth's Birth*, edited by Niger Biggar, 43–57. London: Mowbray, 1988.

Wilson, Jonathan R. *God's Good World: Reclaiming the Doctrine of Creation*. Grand Rapids: Baker Academic, 2013.

Wingren, Gustaf. *Theology in Conflict*. Translated by Eric H. Wahlstrom. Philadelphia: Muhlenberg, 1958.

Young, Norman. *Creator, Creation and Faith*. Philadelphia: Westminster, 1976.

Author Index

Author Index

Subject Index

115

Subject Index

dualism, 28, 30, 45

ecology, 3, 6, 50, 54, 60, 103
Eden, 37, 41
election, 16, 25, 32, 38, 46, 54–56, 61, 77, 85, 89, 91, 95, 97, 99
emanation, 22, 27, 39
Enlightenment, 5, 81
eschatology, 40, 62, 78
essence, 76, 94–95
eternity, 43, 85, 89–90
ethics, 42
existentialism, 5, 69

faith, 3, 6, 8, 11–19, 21, 29, 30, 49
fall, 36, 54, 86–87
Father, 13, 15, 24, 41, 73–82
fellowship, 21–22, 38, 79, 96
filioque, 80, 104
first cause. *See* cause.
freedom, divine, 21–23, 35, 39, 49, 94, 98, 102, 104
freedom, human, 37–39

Garden of Eden. *See* Eden.
gardeners, 60, 64, 104
generation of the Son, 14, 41, 77, 91
Genesis, 10, 24–25, 28, 31, 33, 36, 42, 52, 60, 67, 79
glory, 34–35, 44, 62–63, 104
God, doctrine of, 16, 21–22
goodness of creation, 8, 39, 44–49, 57, 64, 86, 102–3
grace, 24–25, 32–33, 54–56, 78, 85–89, 97–98

heaven, 9, 13–14, 58, 63, 70–71, 81
Hebrews, 11, 28, 30, 76, 93

history, 7, 9–10, 43, 58, 62, 80, 84–91, 96, 100–101
Holy Spirit, 24, 64–65, 67, 73–75, 77–82, 103–4
homoousios, 76
humanity, 6, 13, 25, 28–30, 32–34, 36–38, 50, 52–53, 56–61, 64, 67, 96, 100–101, 103–4

I–Thou, 68–69
image of God, 7, 33, 41, 67–70, 81–82, 95, 104
immanence, 7, 70, 82, 104
incarnation, 39, 63, 91–95, 97
internal basis, 31, 34–38, 44, 49, 51, 55–56, 68, 72, 81, 97, 100–102
Isaiah, 75
Israel, 31, 36–38, 58

Jesus Christ, 3, 5, 7, 11, 13–22, 24–25, 31, 33–34, 38–39, 46–49, 53–56, 58, 61–62, 69, 71, 76–77, 80–82, 84–86, 88–95, 97, 100–104
John, Gospel of, 76, 93

kingdom, 62–63, 93

liberalism, 4–5
liberation, 62, 69
logos asarkos, 77, 84, 91–96, 101, 104
logos ensarkos, 77, 92–93, 101
logos incarnandus, 95
Lord, 16–17, 55, 64, 76, 78, 93, 103
lordship. *See* Lord.

Subject Index

Lightning Source UK Ltd.
Milton Keynes UK
UKOW01f0618140616

276215UK00002B/41/P